Praise for *Learning Chaos Engineering*

Russ Miles explains the theory and practice of chaos engineering in an easy-to-follow tutorial using the Chaos Toolkit. This is a great resource for anyone looking to get started with chaos engineering.

—*Aaron Blohowiak, Engineering Manager at Netflix and coauthor of O'Reilly's* Chaos Engineering *report (http://bit.ly/2VliW0O)*

Exploring systemic weakness in distributed systems is a critical practice for any organization running a cloud-native, microservices-style architecture. This book is a comprehensive and practical guide helping you successfully socialize, implement, and adopt chaos engineering practices. I highly recommend it.

—*Christian Posta, Field CTO, Solo.io*

For anyone who runs production systems, this is a great practical primer on how to get started with using chaos engineering in service of greater confidence in the increasingly complex systems we're building today. You'll learn all the processes and tools you'll need to hit the ground running, even if you've never participated in a Game Day before.

—*Denise Yu, Senior Software Engineer, Pivotal*

Learning Chaos Engineering

Discovering and Overcoming System Weaknesses Through Experimentation

Russ Miles

Beijing · Boston · Farnham · Sebastopol · Tokyo

Learning Chaos Engineering

by Russ Miles

Published by O'Reilly Media, Inc., 1005 Gravenstein Highway North, Sebastopol, CA 95472.

O'Reilly books may be purchased for educational, business, or sales promotional use. Online editions are also available for most titles (*http://oreilly.com*). For more information, contact our corporate/institutional sales department: 800-998-9938 or *corporate@oreilly.com*.

Development Editor: Virginia Wilson	**Indexer:** Ellen Troutman
Acquisitions Editor: Nikki McDonald	**Interior Designer:** David Futato
Production Editor: Katherine Tozer	**Cover Designer:** Karen Montgomery
Copyeditor: Arthur Johnson	**Illustrator:** Rebecca Demarest
Proofreader: Rachel Head	

August 2019:   First Edition

Revision History for the First Edition

2019-07-12:   First Release

See *http://oreilly.com/catalog/errata.csp?isbn=9781492051008* for release details.

978-1-492-05100-8

[LSI]

For my daughter Mali Miles, my own little Chaos Monkey

Table of Contents

Preface

This is a book for *practitioners* of the scientific discipline of chaos engineering. Chaos engineering is part of the overall resilience engineering approach and serves the specific purpose of surfacing evidence of system weaknesses before those weaknesses result in crises such as system outages. If you care about how you, your colleagues, and your entire sociotechnical system collectively practice and respond to threats to your system's reliability, chaos engineering is for you!

Audience

This book is for people who are in some way responsible for their code in production. That could mean developers, operations, DevOps, etc. When I say they "are in some way responsible," I mean that they take responsibility for the availability, stability, and overall robustness of their system as it runs, and may even be part of the group assembled when there is a system outage.

Perhaps you're a site reliability engineer (SRE) looking to improve the stability of the systems you are responsible for, or you're working on a team practicing DevOps where everyone owns their code in production. Whatever your level of responsibility, if you care about how your code runs in production and about the bigger picture of how well production is running for your organization, this book aims to help you meet those challenges.

What This Book Is About

This is a practical guide to doing chaos engineering using free and open source tools, in particular the Chaos Toolkit (see "About the Samples" on page xii). Written by a practitioner, for practitioners, this book introduces the mind-set, the process, the practices, and some of the tools necessary to meet this goal through samples from the open source community, with the specific goal of enabling you to learn how to plan and run successful chaos engineering experiments (see Chapters 3 and 5).

Chaos engineering follows the scientific method, so you'll learn in Part I how to think like a chaos engineering scientist (see Chapter 1), how to come up with a Hypothesis Backlog ready for your chaos experiment exploration (see Chapter 2), and finally, how to develop those valuable hypotheses further into full chaos engineering experiment Game Days (see Chapter 3). Part II helps you make the jump to chaos engineering experiment automation and explore how the chaos engineering learning loop is implemented. Part III brings in the collaborative and operational concerns of chaos engineering (see Chapter 9).

Through this learning path, *Learning Chaos Engineering* aims to give you and your colleagues all you need to begin adopting chaos engineering safely and carefully across your organization right now.

What This Book Is Not About

This book doesn't aim to be the definitive treatment on all the theoretical aspects of chaos engineering, although Chapter 1 does try to distill the essence of the discipline so that you're ready to apply it. It also does not try to be an exhaustive history of the discipline (see *Chaos Engineering* (*https://oreil.ly/2SgxNJf*) by Ali Basiri et al. [O'Reilly]), or even make a guess at the futures of chaos engineering. With minimal fuss, this book tries to cut the fluff and get you practicing chaos engineering successfully as quickly as possible.

About the Samples

All of the chaos experiment automation samples in this book use the free and open source Chaos Toolkit. The Chaos Toolkit is a command-line interface (CLI) and set of extension libraries that enables you to write automated chaos experiments and orchestrate them against your systems.

As part of this book's work, the community has also developed the Chaos Toolkit Community Playground project. This project aims to provide a collection of full-application samples that the community can collaborate around to share experiments, evidence of weaknesses, and even system design improvements out in the open, where everyone can learn from them (see Appendix B).

Conventions Used in This Book

The following typographical conventions are used in this book:

Italic
    Indicates new terms, URLs, email addresses, filenames, and file extensions.

`Constant width`

Used for program listings, as well as within paragraphs to refer to program elements such as variable or function names, databases, data types, environment variables, statements, and keywords.

`Constant width bold`

Shows commands or other text that should be typed literally by the user.

`Constant width italic`

Shows text that should be replaced with user-supplied values or by values determined by context.

 This element signifies a tip or suggestion.

 This element signifies a general note.

 This element indicates a warning or caution.

Using Code Examples

Supplemental material (code examples, exercises, etc.) is available for download at *https://github.com/chaostoolkit-incubator/community-playground*.

This book is here to help you get your job done. In general, if example code is offered with this book, you may use it in your programs and documentation. You do not need to contact us for permission unless you're reproducing a significant portion of the code. For example, writing a program that uses several chunks of code from this book does not require permission. Selling or distributing a CD-ROM of examples from O'Reilly books does require permission. Answering a question by citing this book and quoting example code does not require permission. Incorporating a significant amount of example code from this book into your product's documentation does require permission.

We appreciate, but do not require, attribution. An attribution usually includes the title, author, publisher, and ISBN. For example: "*Learning Chaos Engineering* by Russ Miles (O'Reilly). Copyright 2019 Russ Miles, 978-1-492-05100-8."

If you feel your use of code examples falls outside fair use or the permission given above, feel free to contact us at *permissions@oreilly.com*.

O'Reilly Online Learning

 For almost 40 years, *O'Reilly Media* has provided technology and business training, knowledge, and insight to help companies succeed.

Our unique network of experts and innovators share their knowledge and expertise through books, articles, conferences, and our online learning platform. O'Reilly's online learning platform gives you on-demand access to live training courses, in-depth learning paths, interactive coding environments, and a vast collection of text and video from O'Reilly and 200+ other publishers. For more information, please visit *http://oreilly.com*.

How to Contact Us

Please address comments and questions concerning this book to the publisher:

O'Reilly Media, Inc.
1005 Gravenstein Highway North
Sebastopol, CA 95472
800-998-9938 (in the United States or Canada)
707-829-0515 (international or local)
707-829-0104 (fax)

We have a web page for this book, where we list errata, examples, and any additional information. You can access this page at *https://oreil.ly/learning-chaos*.

Email *bookquestions@oreilly.com* to comment or ask technical questions about this book.

For more information about our books, courses, conferences, and news, see our website at *http://www.oreilly.com*.

Find us on Facebook: *http://facebook.com/oreilly*

Follow us on Twitter: *http://twitter.com/oreillymedia*

Watch us on YouTube: *http://www.youtube.com/oreillymedia*

Acknowledgments

First, I'd like to extend a huge thank you to both Nikki McDonald and Virginia Wilson for helping me get things started, and for shepherding me through all the challenges of writing a book. Thanks also to a fabulous production team that managed to stay sane through the fog of my typos and my accidental disregard for fairly straightforward formatting guidelines. You are all amazingly skilled and have the patience of angels.

Thanks to all the tech reviewers of this book. You gave time from your busy lives to make this book *so* much better; you're more than awesome, and on behalf of all my readers, thank you!

Big thanks to the chaos engineering communities across the world. There are too many names for me to list them all here, but I offer special thanks to Casey and Nora for (along with everyone else) bringing this discipline into the world through the original *Chaos Engineering* ebook (*http://bit.ly/2VliW0O*), and for all of their wonderful talks. Special shout-outs to the Principles of Chaos Engineering (*https://principlesofchaos.org*) and to everyone who puts the effort into maintaining that incredibly important document, and to all those wonderful people who contribute to and use the free and open source Chaos Toolkit!

Thanks to my colleagues at ChaosIQ, especially Sylvain, Marc, and Grant. In particular, a big thanks is in order for all the time Grant spent scratching his head while trying to comprehend my early drafts; thank you for your follicular sacrifice, my friend!

A big thank-you to my family. Mum and Dad, Bobs and Ad (plus Isla and Amber), and Rich and Jo (plus Luke and Leia), you are the best. And finally, Mali, my little girl and the funniest person I know: I hope you keep glowing, munchkin; you make Daddy proud.

Lastly...thank you, dear reader! I hope you enjoy this book, and I look forward to perhaps meeting you in person out on the road somewhere.

Happy chaos engineering!

## PART I

Chaos Engineering Fundamentals

## CHAPTER 1

Chaos Engineering Distilled

Want your system to be able to deal with the knocks and shakes of life in production? Want to find out where the weaknesses are in your infrastructure, platforms, applications, and even people, policies, practices, and playbooks before you're in the middle of a full-scale outage? Want to adopt a practice where you proactively explore weaknesses in your system *before* your users complain? Welcome to chaos engineering.

Chaos engineering is an exciting discipline whose goal is to surface evidence of weaknesses in a system *before* those weaknesses become critical issues. Through tests, you experiment with your system to gain useful insights into how your system will respond to the types of turbulent conditions that happen in production.

This chapter takes you on a tour of what chaos engineering is, and what it isn't, to get you in the right mind-set to use the techniques and tools that are the main feature of the rest of the book.

Chaos Engineering Defined

According to the Principles of Chaos Engineering (*https://principlesofchaos.org*):

> Chaos Engineering is the discipline of experimenting on a system in order to build confidence in the system's capability to withstand turbulent conditions in production.

Users of a system want it to be reliable. *Many* factors can affect reliability (see "Locations of Dark Debt" on page 7), and as chaos engineers we are able to focus on establishing evidence of how resilient our systems are in the face of these unexpected, but inevitable, conditions.

Chaos engineering's sole purpose is to provide evidence of system weaknesses. Through scientific chaos engineering experiments, you can test for evidence of weaknesses in your system—sometimes called *dark debt*—that provides insights into how your system might respond to turbulent, production-like conditions.

Dark Debt?

The STELLA Report (*http://bit.ly/2RDtdBe*) states that "Dark debt is found in complex systems and the anomalies it generates are complex system failures. Dark debt is not recognizable at the time of creation. Its impact is not to foil development but to generate anomalies. It arises from the unforeseen interactions of hardware or software with other parts of the framework. There is no specific countermeasure that can be used against dark debt because it is invisible until an anomaly reveals its presence."

In a nutshell, any sufficiently complex system is likely to contain surprising dark debt that can threaten the functioning of the system. It is a by-product of the necessary complexity of modern software systems and so cannot be designed out. Chaos engineering exists to help you surface evidence of dark debt so that you can meet its challenge before it becomes a critical problem for your system.

Take an example where you have two services that communicate with each other. In Figure 1-1, Service A is dependent on Service B.

Figure 1-1. A simple two-service system

What should happen if Service B dies? What will happen to Service A if Service B starts to respond slowly? What happens if Service B comes back after going away for a period of time? What happens if the connection between Service A and B becomes increasingly busy? What happens if the CPU that is being used by Service B is maxed out? And most importantly, what does this all mean to the user?

You might believe you've designed the services and the infrastructure perfectly to accommodate all of these cases, but how do you know? Even in such a simple system it is likely there might be some surprises—some dark debt—present. Chaos engineering provides a way of exploring these uncertainties to find out whether your assumptions of the system's resiliency hold water in the real world.

What If I Already Know?

I was recently asked, "If I know there's a weakness, that the system will fail if a condition occurs, do I need to do chaos engineering?" It's a fair question, and the immediate answer is no, you don't need chaos engineering if you *know* there's a weakness. Instead, simply prioritize and overcome the weakness. However, sometimes we use the word "know" when we really mean "strongly suspect" or even "believe." That's OK, but chaos engineering can still offer value in such cases because it will provide evidence of the weakness to back up your strong suspicion or belief.

Also, never underestimate the number of weaknesses you may discover when you start to explore something "known." Consider the implementation of a circuit breaker (*http://bit.ly/2LlXSSw*) between the two services shown in Figure 1-1. You could easily state, "We know the system will survive the Service B failure because there is a circuit breaker implemented in Service A," but that's quite the statement of confidence! Do you really *know* what will happen? Do you know how the circuit breaker will respond in all the cases in which Service B's performance degrades? Naively applying resiliency features such as circuit breakers can sometimes cause more problems than not having them at all! Chaos engineering helps here because you can explore these feedback loops and other resiliency capabilities to gather real evidence of how they will respond and affect the rest of the system.

Chaos Engineering Addresses the Whole Sociotechnical System

Chaos engineering doesn't just deal with the technical aspects of your software system; it also encourages exploration across the whole sociotechnical system (Figure 1-2).

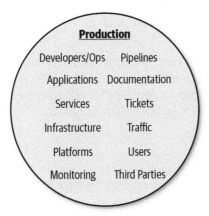

Figure 1-2. Just some of the aspects involved in the entire sociotechnical system

To your organization, chaos engineering is about risk mitigation. A system outage can mean a huge loss of revenue. Even an internal system failing can mean people can't get their jobs done, which is another form of production outage. Chaos engineering helps you explore the conditions of those outages *before* they happen, giving you a chance to overcome those weaknesses before they hit your organization's bottom line.

The reality is that failure in production is "SNAFU."[1] It's only in production that your software comes under the most hostile real-world stresses, and no amount of pre-planning can completely avoid an outage. Chaos engineering takes a different approach. Instead of trying to avoid failure, chaos engineering embraces it.

As a chaos engineer, you build experiments that proactively establish trust and confidence in the resilience of your whole system in production by exploring failure in everything from the infrastructure to the people, processes, and practices involved in keeping the system running and evolving (hint: that's everyone!).

But My Production System Never Fails…

Few production systems *never* fail; even NASA encounters turbulent conditions in "production" on its missions. Just ask Margaret Hamilton, the director of software programming at NASA during the Apollo project. The moon landing would not have happened without her embracing failure.[2] The combination of ever-evolving software, failing hardware, transient network conditions, and *actual users* means that production is a hostile environment in which your code is in fact *most likely* to fail.

Chaos engineering comes with a mind-set that embraces the hostile properties of production systems. I use a lesson taught by my motorcycle instructor to help new chaos engineers get in the groove.

When you are taught to drive a car, you are taught to drive *defensively*. You should always assume that no one else on the road can see you, and that way you will drive with care.

Motorcyclists, on the other hand, are taught that everyone else on the road *can* see them, and they *want them dead*. A motorcyclist should treat other road users, including pedestrians and their dogs, as psychopathic killers whose only reason for traveling is to cause the motorcyclist to be involved in an accident!

---

1 Here I mean "Situation Normal," but the full acronym also applies!

2 See the preface in *Site Reliability Engineering* (*https://oreil.ly/31Ke0ms*), edited by Niall Richard Murphy et al. (O'Reilly), for the full story of how Margaret saved the Apollo moon landing. Once you've read it you'll see why I argue that Margaret Hamilton was a great resilience engineer, and that Margaret's daughter Lauren should be called the "World's First Chaos Engineer!" Tip for parents: the story is also told in the wonderful book, *Margaret and the Moon*, by Dean Robbins (Knopf Books for Young Readers).

This may sound extreme at first, but it works. If you assume everyone is out to get you, then you live a lot longer on that motorcycle. You don't make unfortunate assumptions about how well behaved other road users will be. You don't just ride defensively; you ride with extreme paranoia.

Chaos engineers, and anyone involved in the resilience of production systems, treat production just like a motorcyclist treats the roads and other road users. Production is not passive; it actively wants to ruin your day. Production knows when you're sleeping, when you're on a well-deserved vacation, and especially when you're on a date, and it's just waiting to fall over in fun, interesting, and confusing ways.

Chaos engineers help teams who are responsible for the production systems not forget this fact. Chaos engineering makes the hostile factors of a production environment utterly unignorable and helps teams embrace failure and build more fault-tolerant, robust software and resilient systems. As John Allspaw has tweeted (*http://bit.ly/2XdtgtL*), "Building RESILIENCE is investing in time, attention, and staff to carry out chaos experiments."

Locations of Dark Debt

Dark debt can be present anywhere in a system, but the original chaos engineering tools tended to focus on a system's infrastructure. Netflix's Chaos Monkey (*http://bit.ly/2KHYxOy*), recognized as the first tool in the space, focuses on providing the capability to explore how a system would respond to the death of Amazon Web Services (AWS) EC2 (*https://amzn.to/2YdscCA*) virtual machines in a controlled and random way. Infrastructure, though, is not the only place where dark debt may be.

There are three further broad areas of failure to be considered when exploring your system's potential weaknesses:

- Platform
- Applications
- People, practices, and processes

The infrastructure level encompasses the hardware, your virtual machines, your cloud provider's Infrastructure-as-a-Service (IaaS) features, and the network. The platform level usually incorporates systems such as Kubernetes that work at a higher level of abstraction than infrastructure. Your own code inhabits the application level. Finally, we complete the sociotechnical system that is production by including the people, practices, and processes that work on it.

Dark debt may affect one or more of these areas, in isolation or as a compound effect. This is why you, as a chaos engineer, will consider all of these areas when looking to surface evidence of dark debt across the whole sociotechnical system.

The Process of Chaos Engineering

Chaos engineering begins by asking the question, "Do we *know* what the system might do in this case?" (Figure 1-3). This question could be prompted by a previous incident or might simply spring from the responsible team's worries about one or more cases. Once the question has been asked and is understood to be an important risk to explore (see Chapter 2), the process of chaos engineering can begin.

Figure 1-3. The process of chaos engineering

Starting with your question, you then formulate a hypothesis as the basis for a chaos engineering Game Day or automated chaos experiment (more on this in the next section). The outcomes of those Game Days and chaos experiments will be a collection of observations that provide evidence that one or more weaknesses exist and should be considered as candidates for improvements.

The Practices of Chaos Engineering

Chaos engineering most often starts by defining an experiment that can be run manually by the teams and supported by a chaos engineer. These manual chaos experiments are executed as a Game Day (see Chapter 3) where all the responsible teams and any interested parties can gather to assess how a failure is dealt with "In production" (in fact, when an organization is new to chaos engineering, Game Day experiments are more often executed against a safe staging environment rather than directly in production).

The advantage of Game Days is that they provide a low-technology-cost way to get started with chaos engineering. In terms of time and effort, however, Game Days represent a larger investment from the teams and quickly become unscalable when chaos engineering is done continuously.

You'll want to run chaos experiments as frequently as possible because production is continuously changing, not least through new software deployments and changing user behavior (see Chapter 12). Throw in the fluidity of production running in the cloud, and failure-inducing conditions change from minute to minute, if not second to second! Production conditions aren't called "turbulent" in the definition of chaos engineering for nothing!

Automated chaos engineering experiments come to the rescue here (see Chapter 5). Using your tool of choice, you can carefully automate your chaos experiments so that they can be executed with minimal, or even no manual intervention, meaning you can run them as frequently as you like, and the teams can get on with other work, such as dreaming up new areas of concern for new chaos experiments or even developing and delivering new features.

Sandbox/Staging or Production?

When an organization is in its early stages of maturity in adopting chaos engineering, the temptation to execute experiments against safer, isolated sandbox or staging environments will be strong. Such an approach is not "wrong," but it is worth being aware of the trade-offs.

When considering whether an experiment can be executed in production, it is a good idea to limit its effect—called its *Blast Radius*—as much as possible so as to try to avoid causing a real production incident.[3] The important point is that, regardless of the size of an experiment's Blast Radius, it will not be completely safe. And in fact, it shouldn't be.

Your chaos experiments are attempts to discover and surface new weaknesses. While it's wise to limit the potential known impact of an experiment, the point is still to empirically build trust and confidence that there isn't a weakness, and to do that you are deliberately taking a controlled risk that a weakness—even a big one—may be found.

A good practice is to start with a small–Blast Radius experiment somewhere safer, such as staging, and then grow it's Blast Radius until you are confident the experiment has found no weaknesses in that environment. Then you dial back the Blast Radius again as you move the experiment to production so that you can begin to discover weaknesses there instead.

Running a Game Day or an automated chaos experiment in staging or some other safe(r) environment has the upside of not interrupting the experience of the system's real users should the experiment get out of control, but it has the downside of not discovering real evidence of the weakness being present in production. It is this evidence in production that gives a chaos experiment's findings their unignorable power to encourage improvement in the system's resilience that can be lost when a weakness is found "just in staging."

---

3 Adrian Hornsby, Senior Technology Evangelist at AWS, said at a talk that "Chaos Engineers should obsess about blast radius."

Production Brings Learning Leverage

I try to encourage organizations to at least consider how they might, in as safe a way as possible, eventually graduate their experiments into production because of the need to make the findings from the chaos experiments as unignorable as possible. After all, in production *everyone* can hear you scream…

Chaos Engineering and Observability

While *any* system can benefit right away from immediately applying chaos engineering in small ways, there is at least one important system property that your chaos engineering experiments will rely upon almost immediately: observability.

Charity Majors (*https://twitter.com/mipsytipsy*) describes observability as a running system's ability to be debugged. The ability to comprehend, interrogate, probe, and ask questions of a system *while it is running* is at the heart of this debuggability.

Chaos engineering—particularly automated chaos experiments—encourages and relies on the observability of the system so that you're able to detect the evidence of your system's reactions to the turbulent conditions caused by your experiments. Even if you do not have good system observability when you begin to adopt chaos engineering, you will quickly see the value and need for system debuggability in production. Thus, chaos engineering and observability frequently go hand in hand with each other, chaos engineering being one forcing factor to improve your system's observability.

Is There a "Chaos Engineer"?

Chaos engineering is a technique that everyone in the team responsible for software in production will find useful. Just as writing tests is something everyone is responsible for, so thinking about experiments and conducting Game Days and writing automated chaos experiments is a job best done as part of the regular, day-to-day work of everyone in the team. In this way, everyone is a chaos engineer, and it is more of an additional skill than a full-time role.

Some large companies, like Netflix, do employ full-time chaos engineers—but their jobs are not quite what you'd expect. These individuals work with the software-owning teams to support them by doing chaos engineering through workshops, ideation, and tooling. Sometimes they also coordinate larger chaos experiments across multiple teams. What they don't do is attack other people's systems with surprise chaos experiments of their own. That wouldn't be science; that would be sadism!

So while chaos engineering is a discipline that everyone can learn with practice, your company may have a dedicated set of chaos engineers supporting the teams, and even a dedicated resilience engineering group. The most important thing is that everyone is aware of, and has bought into chaos experiments and has an opportunity to learn from their findings.

Summary

The goal of this chapter was to distill as much of the discipline of chaos engineering as possible so that you will be able to successfully begin creating, running, and learning from your own chaos engineering experiments. You've learned what chaos engineering is useful for and how to *think* like a chaos engineer.

You've also gotten an overview of the practices and techniques that comprise chaos engineering in Game Days and automated chaos experiments. Finally, you've learned how the role of chaos engineer successfully works within and alongside teams.

That's enough about what chaos engineering *is*—now it's time to take your first steps towards applying the discipline by learning how to source, capture, and prioritize your first set of chaos engineering experiment hypotheses.

## CHAPTER 2

Building a Hypothesis Backlog

The aim of chaos engineering is to help you build trust and confidence in how your whole sociotechnical system will perform during turbulent conditions. One way to get rolling might be to jump straight in and start introducing those turbulent conditions—break networks, introduce latency, and see what collapses[1]

But wait! Before you unleash Chaos Monkey unchained (*http://bit.ly/2KHYxOy*) in production, remember that you want to *learn* from your chaos, which means that you need much more than just to have *caused* chaos. You need to follow the scientific method.

How NOT to Do Chaos Engineering

Chaos Monkey unchained might sound fun, interesting, or plain frightening, depending on your experience. In this case, it happens to be a real case study of exactly how *not* to do chaos engineering…

I received a call from a client that started like this:

Client: "We're considering doing chaos engineering and might need some of your help…"

Me: "OK, what can we help you with?"

Client: "We've just run Chaos Monkey…"

Me: "OK…"

Client: "… in production."

---

1 You could do this in production, if you're feeling especially masochistic…

Me: "Oh… so you've been doing this for a while?"

Client: "It broke everything."

Me: "Ah."

Client: "We knew it would…"

Me: "OK, I think you should stop—you're not actually being chaos engineers…"

Chaos engineering is not just about breaking things, and if that's what you aim for, then all that will result is pain for you and your users! This is *exactly* why we say that chaos engineering is a controlled, disciplined scientific approach. As chaos engineers we start with "What do we want to learn?" and not "What can we break first?"

Start with Experiments?

If chaos engineering follows the scientific method, then starting with an experiment seems like the right choice. The challenge then quickly becomes, "Which experiment?" Experiments are often complex and detailed, and, more importantly, require a lot of work to plan and execute. That's a big expenditure of wasted effort should you ultimately decide not to conduct the experiment.

A better approach is to take a step back to figure out what experiments you might find valuable *before* you go ahead and invest your time and effort.

What Experiments Would Build Trust and Confidence?

Chaos engineering does not start with the question, "Where shall we create chaos?", but rather with, "Where would it be most valuable to create an experiment that helps us build trust and confidence in our system under turbulent conditions?"

Instead of starting by injecting failure and chaos, or even by designing full-blown experiments, start by asking "What idea do we want to gather some evidence to support or refute?" or more simply, "What could possibly go wrong?" These questions are the essence of a hypothesis, and so the key to figuring out what experiments to invest in starts with building up a backlog of such questions for your own systems. This collection of questions is called the *Hypothesis Backlog*.

Gathering Hypotheses

There are *many* sources of hypotheses when it comes to how a system might deviate from the norm, such as:

- Conducting past incident analysis
- Asking "What could happen if…?" or "What worries us?" ideally using a common, detailed sketch of the system

We'll look at incident analysis and sketching the system next.

Incident Analysis

Incident analysis is a whole body of work, even a field in itself, that touches on many aspects of safety and how humans think and operate in challenging situations. It deserves a book in its own right! From the perspective of chaos engineering, identifying contributing causes through incident analysis is fertile ground for starting to think about hypotheses for chaos experiments.

But in many respects, it's like the age-old saying of "locking the stable door after the horse has bolted." Learning from past incidents is an essential job for any team that is investing in resilience, and chaos engineering can help with that learning by providing additional evidence of weaknesses as the system is improved. However, learning *only* from past incidents is a "postmortem" approach and is frequently expensive and painful. Using only this learning approach, you are naturally reactive, making decisions based on evidence sourced from the harshest of situations and conditions.

Instead of relying solely on incident analysis, chaos engineering offers us a much more proactive approach; think of it as *pre*-mortem.

Sketching Your System

Start by sketching your system. Get your team together and come up with a picture of your system, including all the people, practices, and processes involved, that describes in detail what the system looks like.[2]

You want your system sketch, or sketches, to be detailed enough that you can start to ask specific questions about what could be explored. The sketch is your first step toward building a sensitivity to failure in your system. This sensitivity is by no means

---

2 I suggest using the guidelines for sketching the technical facets of systems that Simon Brown describes in his excellent "C4: Context, Containers, Components and Code" approach (*https://c4model.com/*).

special to chaos engineering, but it is something that you will develop as a skill over time as you gain more experience with the practice.

Examples, Sketches and Source

A set of sketches and source code for an example application is provided and is being developed and contributed to by the Chaos Toolkit community (*https://chaostoolkit.org*) in its Community Playground project on GitHub (*http://bit.ly/2JbI6a7*) for you to grab, run, and even contribute to. See Appendix B for information on this project.

We recommend getting your own copy of the project, even if only so you can peruse the code as you learn chaos engineering throughout this book.

You will very likely end up with more than one sketch, and it's common to have at least one for each of the different areas where dark debt may be present in your system. Here are some examples of questions to ask with regard to each potential area of dark debt:

People, practices, and processes
Who works with the system? What continuous integration and delivery (CI/CD) pipeline do you have, and with what stages? What monitoring systems do you have, and who is responsible for them?

Application
What are the timeouts configured at the application level? Are there any persistence systems you are integrating with?

Platform
What platform services is your system relying on or providing? Is a container orchestration layer such as Kubernetes (*https://kubernetes.io*) being used?

Infrastructure
What virtual machines, actual machines, networks, racks, servers, etc., are in place?

The secret here is to go as deep and be as detailed as you can, while making sure your system sketches are something that everyone recognizes so that you can achieve an accurate baseline picture before asking the all-important question, "What do we want to explore?"

Refining Mental Models

The value of this process of collectively sketching out your entire sociotechnical system cannot be underestimated. It's often best to do it in a way that can be maintained over time. You are capturing and clarifying everyone's mental models of the system; this is valuable because sharing and refining mental models is one reason some teams can move quickly and with confidence when working with, and even developing and evolving, their software-based systems.[3]

Capturing "What Could Possibly Go Wrong?"

With your system sketches now in hand you can ask these questions:

- "Could this fail?"
- "Has this caused problems before?"
- "If this fails, what else could be impacted?"

Any question that helps you explore the possibilities for failure in your system is a good one at this stage. You won't be able to spot them all, and that's OK. At this point what's important is just to build up a big collection of possible failures.

You Won't Catch Them All...Ever

It's in the nature of complex systems that you won't be able to identify every potential failure with only a diagram and a conversation. Even after prolonged running of the system, and explorations with chaos experiments, a system can still surprise you. Chaos engineering helps you to explore as many potential surprises before time as possible, but it doesn't guarantee you have the perfect system. This is another reason why chaos engineering never ends—it is a practice that you will apply for the entire lifetime of your system, from its original design and inception through to the day it is all turned off.

Write down each failure you and the team highlight, making sure to describe it in as much detail as you can. Figure 2-1 shows an example of a failure card.

---

3 Jessica Kerr (*http://bit.ly/2Xtt191*) talks and writes often about the value of understanding and developing shared mental models and how this contributes to high-performing teams.

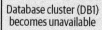

Figure 2-1. Failure card

Collectively, you and your team will come up with many, *many* possible failures through this exercise alone, especially when you consider all the different levels of attack and their compound effects. Take your time with this important step. It is an opportunity not only to find failures but to really build that sensitivity to failure that is crucial to a chaos engineer.

Introducing Likelihood and Impact

At some point you will begin to exhaust your team's ideas, or perhaps your list will start to feel endless. A big list of failures is a scary thing and is not very helpful on its own, but with a little more work you can turn it into what you need.

To turn your collection of failures into something more useful you are going to apply a technique called Failure Mode and Effects Analysis *Lite*. Failure Mode and Effects Analysis (*http://bit.ly/2NhR5vU*) is a powerful technique that has long been part of a reliability engineer's toolbox.[4] You are going to use a faster version of the technique purely for the refinement of your set of failures, to help you decide which failures should be turned into chaos engineering hypotheses for your backlog.

So far you've completed the first two steps of building a Hypothesis Backlog:

- Build a detailed sketch of your system.
- Brainstorm and collect a set of detailed possible system failures across your real system and from the perspective of different attack vectors.

The next step is:

- Understand, discuss, map out, and agree on the relative likelihood and impact of those failures.

---

4 Thanks to Jenny Martin for all the insights about how this process could be tailored to chaos engineering.

Building a Likelihood-Impact Map

Your collection of potential failures needs a little spice to make it really useful. The spice you'll add in now includes:

- The likelihood that a failure may occur[5]
- The potential impact your system will experience if it does

You can factor in this information to build a *likelihood-impact map.*

Isn't Likelihood Just Guesswork?

In many respects, the level of probability that you'll consider for your likelihood-impact map is just guesswork, and that's as far as it needs to go at this point. You don't actually know the real impact of even posited failures such as the ones in your big list; that's something that chaos engineering experiments will help you find evidence for once you've decided which ones are worth the effort of making them into experiments.

First, if you haven't already done so, put each detailed failure on its own card or sticky note. Then create a large grid with the labels "Impact" and "Likelihood" on it, as shown in Figure 2-2.[6]

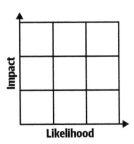

Figure 2-2. Empty impact and likelihood grid

Now take each of your specific failure cards or sticky notes and collectively, as a team, discuss where on the map it should be placed. If it's a high-likelihood failure—perhaps one you've seen frequently—with a large impact on customer or user experience,

---

5 I use "likelihood" here rather than "probability" as what we are discussing is far from formal, mathematical probability.

6 Using as big a whiteboard as you can possibly find, or maybe even an available wall, is great for this exercise. It will ideally be something you can keep permanently as your "Wall of Failure Sensitivity."

then it should go toward the top right corner of the map. If it's something you hardly ever expect to see—and something that would likely have little impact on the user experience of your system if it did arise—then the bottom left corner would be the right place for it.

Continue placing your failures onto the map until you and your team have something like the grid shown in Figure 2-3.

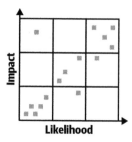

Figure 2-3. Failure cards arranged on impact and likelihood grid

All Big-and-Likely or All Low-and-Unlikely?

Any group of people can have a collective bias toward optimism or pessimism. This means the group might have all of its failures clustered in the bottom right section, or in the top left section. For instance, if this exercise were carried out by a team with a natural tendency toward optimism, the map might look like Figure 2-4.

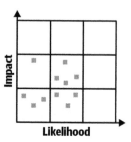

Figure 2-4. Perhaps an optimistic arrangement of failure cards

One response to this is simply to leave the map as it is; after all, it is not wrong per se —it is just one group's perspective. If you're unhappy with having such a map, though, there is an easy solution: adjust the scale of the map to give you a better spread, as Figure 2-5 shows.

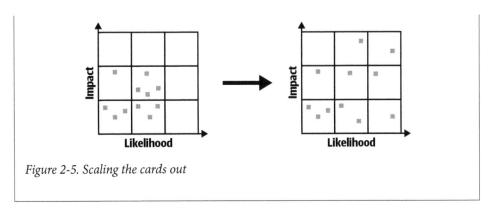

Figure 2-5. Scaling the cards out

You now have a picture of what failures are guessed to be most likely, and an estimate of their potential impact on the user experience. You might feel at this point that you have enough to start building a plan for applying chaos to explore some of your potential failure cases—but wait! There is one final step that will make this map even more useful to you in figuring out what failures to work into chaos experiment hypotheses. It's time to figure out which failures might actually affect what you care about the most.

Adding What You Care About

You have a map full of potentially worrying failures, organized by your own guesses as to their likelihood and potential impact. You need one more bit of information to turn them into a collection you can navigate and pick from when building your Hypothesis Backlog: an estimate of what the value would be to you and your team, and even your organization, if you were to build trust and confidence in how the system reacts to a particular failure.

This might sound like a complicated thing to add, but it's usually simpler than you think, though it does require thought and discussion. You need to build another list of the things you, your team, and your company care about. Call it a "taxonomy of - ilities."[7] Ask "What do we care about?" and you'll likely come up with a list that includes the following:

- Reliability
- Safety
- Security
- Durability

_____

7 Mainly because a lot of the things you care about will end with "-ility."

- Availability

Some of these may require discussion within the team about what everyone thinks the term might mean for your context, but as long as you all agree, then your list is fine regardless of what it contains. It is *your* list of things you care about.

Some Failure Conditions Are Acceptable

Some failures are acceptable even when their impact is significant. While you are working through your failures, it is worth asking about each one: "Is this acceptable?" If it is, then labeling it with the keyword "Acceptable" means you have declared that this failure may not be worth investing the time and effort to explore through chaos engineering.

Now take another look at each of the failures on your map and mark what "-ilities" you think might be affected if that failure happened. Once again, these are guesses, and it's not wrong to conclude that every failure will affect all of the things you care about. When you're done, each failure will look like the example shown in Figure 2-6.

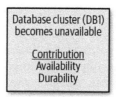

Figure 2-6. Failure card with contribution added

You now have a collective understanding of:

- What failures you can guess might happen
- What impact you can guess a particular failure might have
- What likelihood you guess a failure might have of occurring
- What things you care about might be affected if a given failure occurs

This means that you now have everything you need to take the final step: creating your Hypothesis Backlog!

Creating Your Hypothesis Backlog

A chaos experiment starts with a hypothesis, and with everything you've already prepared, the next steps should be easy—not just converting a failure into a hypothesis in

---

a backlog, but also prioritizing which hypotheses might be worth taking to the next level by turning them into a full chaos experiment for a Game Day (see Chapter 3) or even a fully automated chaos experiment (see Chapters Chapter 4 and Chapter 5).

Discuss with your team which failures are worth making into hypotheses. You should have all you need to make that decision, based on combinations such as:

- Selecting the high-impact, high-likelihood failures that map most closely to the most important "ilities"
- Selecting the lowest-impact failures so that you can explore chaos engineering as safely as possible
- Selecting the failures that have the most "-ilities," and therefore perhaps the greatest value, to be explored further

Your map of failures supplies the raw data. It is now up to you and your team to decide what criteria for selection to apply. Eventually you will have a subset of failures to focus on, and converting them into hypotheses simply requires you to shift the terminology of the failure from "what happens and its impact" to "when it happens it will not have the impact."

For example, take the failure card from Figure 2-6. You can convert that into a hypothesis card by switching the emphasis as demonstrated in Figure 2-7.

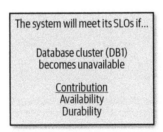

Figure 2-7. Hypothesis card

Now your newly minted hypothesis card reads: "The system will meet its SLOs if database cluster (DB1) becomes unavailable," where SLO stands for Service Level Objective. This hypothesis is worth considering for prioritizing as an experiment because of where the card is placed on the likelihood-impact map (a high-impact failure), and because of its importance in contributing to building trust and confidence in your system in terms of the "-ilities:" durability and availability.

Summary

Grab a beverage—you've come a long way! In this chapter you've learned how to build a catalog of potential failures and—adding impact, likelihood, and value ("-ilities")—turn those failures into a set of prioritized hypotheses in a backlog that are ready for consideration as chaos engineering experiments.

Once you've recharged, it will be time to take one of those hypotheses and explore it in the simplest (and cheapest, in terms of tooling) way possible, through planning and running a Game Day.

## CHAPTER 3

Planning and Running a Manual Game Day

How many times have you heard comments like the following after a production incident?

"We were not prepared for *that*!"

"Dashboards were lighting up, we didn't know where to look..."

"Alarms were going off, and we didn't know why..."

The absolute worst time to try and learn about the weaknesses in your sociotechnical system is during an incident. There's panic; there's stress; there may even be anger. It's hardly the time to be the person that suggests, "Shall we just step back a moment and ask ourselves how this all happened?" "It's a little too late, it's happening!" would be the reply, if you're lucky and people are feeling inordinately polite.

Chaos engineering has the single goal of helping you collect evidence of system weaknesses *before* those weaknesses become incidents. While no guarantees can be made that you'll ever find every one of the multitude of compound potential weaknesses in a system, or even just all the catastrophic ones, it is good engineering sense to be proactive about exploring your system's weaknesses ahead of time.

So far you have hypotheses of how your system should respond in the event of turbulent conditions. The next step is to grab some tools and start breaking things in production, right? Wrong!

The cheapest way[1] to get started with chaos engineering requires no tools. It requires your effort, your time, your team's time, and ideally the time of anyone who has a stake in your system's reliability. Effort and time are all you need to plan and run a Game Day.

---

1 Cheapest in terms of tooling, not in terms of time.

What Is a Game Day?

A Game Day is a practice event, and although it *can* take a whole day, it usually requires only a few hours. The goal of a Game Day is to practice how you, your team, and your supporting systems deal with real-world turbulent conditions. You collectively get to explore:

- How well your alerting systems perform
- How your team members react to an incident
- Whether you have any indication that your system is healthy or not
- How your technical system responds to the turbulent conditions

A Game Day is not just a random event in which things break; it is a controlled, safe, and observed experiment through which you can collect evidence of how your sociotechnical system responds to the turbulent conditions that underpin your chaos engineering hypothesis. At its most basic it doesn't require any tools at all—just a plan, a notepad and pen, and an awareness of what is going on and just how much you can learn from it!

A Game Day turns a hypothesis from your backlog into an experiment you can execute with your team to rapidly surface weaknesses in your entire sociotechnical system. You deliberately practice (*http://bit.ly/2NjHZP5*) for unexpected conditions and capture evidence of any weaknesses in how you, your team, and your supporting systems deal with those conditions, choosing what to learn from and improve over time.

Planning Your Game Day

A Game Day can take any form you want as long as it ends up providing detailed and accurate evidence of system weaknesses. As you gain experience planning and running Game Days, you are likely to come up with all sorts of ideas about how you can improve the quality of your findings. For your first few Game Days, the following steps will help you get started successfully:

1. Pick a hypothesis to explore.
2. Pick a style.
3. Decide who participates in your Game Day and who observes.
4. Decide where your Game Day is going to happen.
5. Decide when your Game Day is going to start, and how long it will last.
6. Describe your Game Day experiment.
7. Get approval!

As you work through this chapter, you will build and then learn how to execute a Game Day plan—but before you can get started, you'll need to pick a valuable hypothesis to explore during your Game Day.

Pick a Hypothesis

Trying to decide what to explore in a Game Day can be a pain if all you have to go on is what people tell you worries them. Everyone will have different pet concerns, and all of those concerns are valid. As a Game Day is not inexpensive in terms of time and effort, you will feel the pressure to ensure that the time and attention are spent on something as *valuable* as possible.

If you created a Hypothesis Backlog earlier (see "Creating Your Hypothesis Backlog" on page 22), then you're in a much better place. The hypotheses in your ever-changing and expanding backlog make it as easy as possible to collectively decide what to invest a Game Day in, as each one describes:

- How you hope the system will respond
- The turbulent conditions that could be involved (failures, traffic spikes, etc.)
- The collective feel for how likely these turbulent conditions might be
- The collective feel for how big an impact these conditions might have on the system (although the hypothesis should be that the system will survive in some fashion)
- The valuable system qualities that you hope to build trust and confidence in by exploring the hypothesis

Together with your team and stakeholders, you can use these hypothesis descriptions to reach agreement on one that is valuable enough to explore in a Game Day. Then it's time to consider the type of Game Day you are looking to perform.

Pick a Style of Game Day

Game Days come in an ever-increasing set of styles and formats. They tend to vary in terms of how much prior information is shared with the participants, and thus in what the scope might be for surfacing evidence of weaknesses in the system. A couple of popular Game Day styles are:

Dungeons & Dragons
    Where none of the participants are aware of the conditions they are walking into

Informed in Advance
    Where the participants are told before the Game Day about the type of incident they are walking into

Picking a Game Day style is not just a question of taste. It's important to consider what evidence you are likely to find if applying one style versus another. For example, an adversarial Dungeons & Dragons–style Game Day in which no one is aware of the actual problem beforehand will explore:

- How the team detects turbulent conditions
- How the team diagnoses turbulent conditions
- How the team responds to turbulent conditions

An Informed in Advance–style Game Day will likely be limited to showing how the participants respond to turbulent conditions.

Decide Who Participates and Who Observes

Deciding who will attend is one of the most important steps in planning your Game Day, but possibly not for the reason you'd expect. You might think that the more important decision is who is going to participate in your Game Day, but that's usually straightforward: you invite your team and anyone else who would likely be involved if the turbulent conditions of your hypothesis were to happen "for real." Add all of those names to your "Invite List"—see Figure 3-1.

Invite List

Name	Role (participant/ observer)	Reason

Figure 3-1. Game Day participants and observers list

Then it's time to consider the second—and just as important—group for your Game Day: the people who are going to *observe* it.

This list should include everyone who might have any interest in the findings. Think broadly when compiling your observers list, from the CEO on down! You are trying to increase the awareness of the findings for your Game Day.

Decide Where

There are two things to decide when it comes to the question of "where" of your Game Day:

- Where will everyone be?
- Where will the turbulent conditions occur?

Ideally, the answer to the first question is "where they would be if the actual conditions occurred for real." The second question is harder to answer. You could conduct the Game Day experiment by applying the turbulent conditions in production, but… you don't want this Game Day to accidentally turn into a real incident![2]

Often Game Day experiments limit their Blast Radius (the potential real-world impact of the experiment) to a safer environment than production, such as a staging environment. Nothing beats production for giving you the best possible evidence of real weaknesses, but if you run a Game Day and you take down production, that just might be the last bit of chaos engineering you'll be asked to do!

Running Your Game Day Somewhere Safe(r)

There's no doubt that performing Game Days—even the automated chaos experiments that you'll learn about in Part III—in production, where there are real users, is how you are likely to learn the most. It's also possible that some experiments can't be simulated anywhere else due to conditions and scale needs.

However, it's usually best to start executing your experiments in a safer environment with a small Blast Radius and then to scale up gradually with larger and larger Blast Radii, gaining trust and confidence in your system's ability to handle the conditions, before you go anywhere near production with the experiment.

Decide When and For How Long

A Game Day experiment can take up an entire day, but don't be afraid to make it a lot less than a whole day either. Even just three hours is a long time to be in a crisis situation, and don't think that there won't be huge amounts of stress involved just because your participants know the issue is in a "safe" staging environment.

You should plan your Game Day for when you anticipate that the participants and observers are going to be most open to, and even eager to learn from, its findings—for example, before a team retrospective.

If your team does retrospectives regularly, then it's often a great idea to execute your Game Days just before them. This very neatly helps to avoid the problem of having dull retrospectives—nothing beats dullness like walking into a retrospective armed

---

2 See "Consider a "Safety Monitor"" on page 32 for how this can happen even when you don't plan to use the production environment on Game Day.

with an emotionally fraught set of evidence of system weaknesses just experienced during a Game Day!

Describe Your Game Day Experiment

Now it's time to construct your Game Day experiment. The experiment will include:

A steady-state hypothesis
> A set of measurements that indicate that the system is working in an expected way from a business perspective, and within a given set of tolerances

A method
> The set of activities you're going to use to inject the turbulent conditions into the target system

Rollbacks
> A set of remediating actions through which you will attempt to repair what you have done knowingly in your experiment's method

So far you have a backlog of hypotheses, but the emphasis of a *steady-state hypothesis* is a little different from the hypothesis card shown earlier in Figure 2-7.

"Steady-state" means that you can measure that the system is working in an expected way. In this case, that normal behavior is that "the system will meet its SLOs." You need to decide what measurement, with what tolerance, would indicate that your system was in fact responding in this timely fashion. For example, you could decide to probe the system on a particular URL and ensure that the system responds with a tolerance that included an expected HTTP status code and within a given time that was set by a Service Level Objective.[3]

There might be multiple measurements that collectively indicate that your system is behaving, within tolerance, in a normal way. These measurements should be listed, along with their tolerances, as your Game Day's steady-state hypothesis—see Figure 3-2.

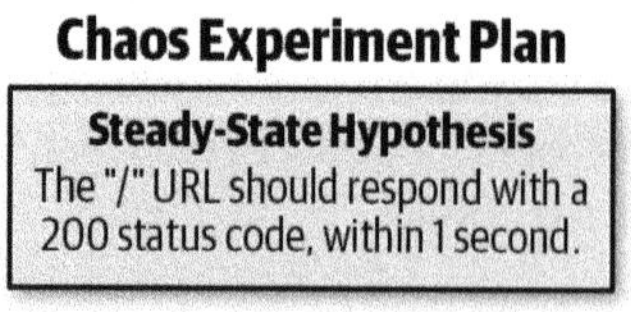

Chaos Experiment Plan

> **Steady-State Hypothesis**
> The "/" URL should respond with a 200 status code, within 1 second.

Figure 3-2. Chaos experiment steady-state hypothesis

---

3 Find more on how to set SLOs in *Site Reliability Engineering* (*https://oreil.ly/31Ke0ms*), by Niall Richard Murphy et al. (O'Reilly).

Next, you need to capture what you're going to do to your system to cause the turbulent conditions, and when you are going to perform those actions within the duration of your Game Day. This collection of actions is called the experiment's *method*, and it should read as a list of actions that cause all the failures and other turbulent conditions you need to create for your Game Day—see Figure 3-3.

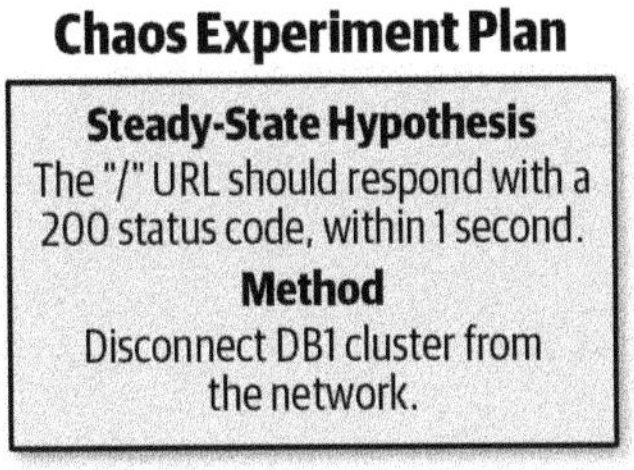

Chaos Experiment Plan

Steady-State Hypothesis
The "/" URL should respond with a
200 status code, within 1 second.
Method
Disconnect DB1 cluster from
the network.

Figure 3-3. Chaos experiment method

Finally, you capture a list of remediating actions—or rollbacks as they are usually called—that you can perform to put things back the way they were, to the best of your ability, because you *know* you caused problems in those areas when you executed the actions in your experiment's method (see Figure 3-4).

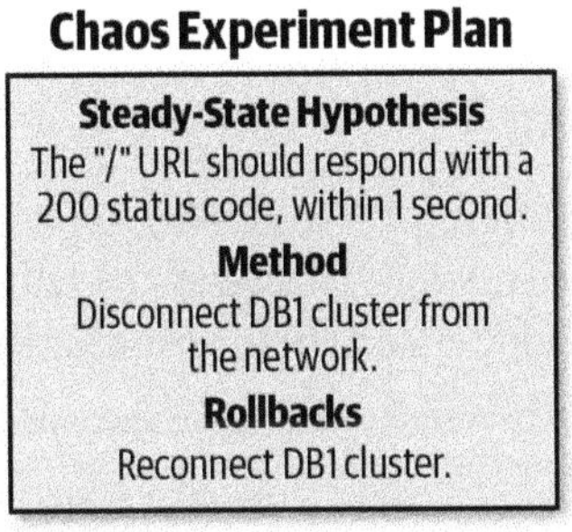

Chaos Experiment Plan

Steady-State Hypothesis
The "/" URL should respond with a
200 status code, within 1 second.
Method
Disconnect DB1 cluster from
the network.
Rollbacks
Reconnect DB1 cluster.

Figure 3-4. Chaos experiment complete with rollbacks

Get Approval!

Last but never least, make sure that you create a list of people who will need to be notified and approve of running the Game Day. This could be everyone from the CEO to up- or downstream systems, and on through to third-party users of the system. Add to your Game Day plan a "notifications and approvals" table (see Figure 3-5) and make sure you've chased everyone down before the Game Day is announced.

Notifications and Approvals

Name	Role	Approved?
Bob Jennifer	Owner CEO	✓

Figure 3-5. Table of notifications and approvals

Running the Game Day

Your job when running your Game Day is to adopt the role of "Game Day facilitator." This means that you aren't a participant. Your job is to keep a detailed log of everything that happens so that this record can be used to elicit weaknesses after the event. Feel free to use every piece of technology or trick you can think of to record as many observations as possible during the Game Day; you never know what might lead to an interesting finding. For example, a participant staring off into space for 20 minutes might appear to be of no interest, but if you make a note of it and then ask them about it afterwards, you might find out that they were thinking, "I don't even know where to start to look," which *is* valuable information.

Consider a "Safety Monitor"

Sometimes you might be facilitating a Game Day experiment against a system that you have little personal knowledge of. This tends to happen when you are asked to help another team begin to adopt chaos engineering. If this is the case, be aware that you might need a "Safety Monitor."[4]

A Safety Monitor is likely the most experienced expert on the system that is being used for the Game Day. You have to accept the compromise that they will not be a participant but will be working closely with you, the facilitator, instead. Their job is to alert you if the Game Day is going in a dangerous direction.

For instance, imagine that you planned for the Game Day to be exercised in a safe staging environment, but the team accidentally starts to diagnose and manipulate production. The Safety Monitor, with their expert knowledge of the system, will likely

---

4 You might need one regardless; in fact, always consider the possibility.

detect this sort of dangerous deviation and can advise you to halt the Game Day before any damage occurs beyond the expected Blast Radius of the experiment.

The Case of the Lucky Game Day Facilitator

I was feeling great. I suspected (strongly) that there was a weakness in the system, and his name was "Bob."[5] Bob was a hero, and it was easy to spot. Ask anyone on the team how something was done in production, or even in staging, and the answer was usually "See Bob," or at least "Better see Bob to check."

Many teams have Bobs—heroes that end up being single points of knowledge and failure. It's not always their fault, either; sometimes they are simply the person who has been around the longest, or the one who was able to most quickly build a mental model of the system. Bobs happen all the time, and you probably know of one in your own team—but this doesn't take away from the fact that Bob is a weakness, because he (or she) is a single point of knowledge.

Now I wanted proof. I wanted to make this potential weakness in the system unignorable by everyone. I could just tell everyone that Bob was a single point of failure, but that tactic more often than not results in a shrug and a "Yeah, we should do better at that…" I wanted people to *feel* the problem, and the best way to explore this was with a chaos engineering Game Day.

So I asked Bob's boss if I could kill Bob. In fact, the question I posed was, "Can Bob go under the proverbial bus?" It may sound nasty, but I was simply asking whether I could run a Game Day in which Bob was totally and utterly out of action. Not present, virtually or otherwise—complete disconnection. After I clarified to Bob's boss that I wasn't actually looking to commit murder, the plan was agreed to.

When I spoke to Bob, he was on board with the plan, with one condition: I had to phone his wife and explain that he would be completely out of contact for the three-hour Game Day. I'd made it clear that he had to disconnect because there was every chance the team might resort to calling him, so it had to look like a complete shutdown of all communications with Bob for this to work. Fortunately, Bob's wife was quite keen on him "going under the bus," which I chose not to explore with any more questions.

The Game Day was planned and scheduled. Bob took his place in an adjoining room with no connectivity. I introduced some turbulent conditions in the staging environment and briefed the team that we were doing a Game Day against staging. The first reaction from the team was perfect: "We can't do the Game Day, Bob isn't here." Yes! That's just what I expected, and I gently encouraged everyone to continue regardless.

---

5 Yes, the name has been changed to protect the innocent.

Now, let's skip to the middle of the Game Day. It was around two hours in, and the team was clearly struggling but making ground. They didn't know where the playbooks were (noted as a weakness), and they had a nightmare trying to get hold of passwords so that they could start probing the system to figure out what was going on (also duly noted); however, they seemed busy, and the atmosphere was one of progress.

But I was nervous. I'd seen a lot of actions being taken without consulting the playbooks or any other reference material. Commands were often being executed with a precursory muttering of "Let's just try this..." That might have been fine, but I was starting to feel nervous about the limits of my own knowledge of the system. I was worried about something being done that I wasn't smart enough to stop.

I was starting to feel that even *I* needed Bob.

So I began popping over to the adjacent room and running some questions by Bob. I mentioned some commands and parameters being used and asked whether these sounded at all right. Then before I could continue further with my questions, Bob leaped off his seat, barreled past me, and announced with a shout of horror, "Stop!"

The Game Day was suspended immediately. It turned out the team had logged into the wrong system—production, in fact—and were in the process of destroying tables in the production database. They had no idea they'd headed to the wrong target, and were flummoxed as to why the system seemed "fine" when the dashboards were actually reporting turbulent conditions. Fortunately for me and the team, I'd followed my gut and spoken to Bob in time to stop major damage being done.

We learned a lot from this Game Day—the list of observations of weaknesses in knowledge, practices, tooling, playbooks, etc. just went on and on. But the biggest lesson of all was for me. Bob had been my impromptu "Safety Monitor," and I'd never again conduct a Game Day without a Bob at hand.

Oh, and Bob was indeed a single point of failure, and *everyone* had felt that pain. In the ensuing retrospective, dedicated plans were put in place to begin to increase everyone's knowledge of the runtime system, with Bob's full endorsement. In fact, he'd been mentioning for ages how he'd like to train people up, but only now was the motivation there for this to actually happen. One of the observers of the Game Day was the product owner, who was only too happy to dedicate the time and budget to this as well.

Mission accomplished—but perhaps a much riskier lesson to learn than I would have liked.

Summary

In this chapter you learned how to build and run your first chaos experiment as a manual Game Day. Game Days are very useful for exploring weaknesses collaboratively. If the Game Day is properly planned, the findings are hard to ignore, and you can achieve much with this relatively small investment in time and effort. Game Days are also perfect for exploring the human side of the system, which is where a huge amount of system weaknesses are often found.

However, Game Days are cheap in tooling but not in time and effort, so there are limitations when it comes to how often you can plan and run them. Each Game Day will help to build more trust and confidence in how your sociotechnical team will react to turbulent conditions, but if you can execute a Game Day only once a week, month, or quarter, then that's the limit of how often you can learn from weaknesses. In the next part of the book, you're going to learn how you can overcome these limitations of Game Days by creating automated chaos experiments.

## PART II

Chaos Engineering Automation

## CHAPTER 4

Getting Tooled Up for Automated Chaos Engineering

Automated chaos experiments give you the power to potentially explore system weaknesses at any time. There are many turbulent condition–inducing tools out there, from the original Netflix Chaos Monkey for infrastructure-level chaos, to application-level tools such as the Chaos Monkey for Spring Boot. Here you are going to use the Chaos Toolkit (*https://chaostoolkit.org*) and its ecosystem of extensions.

The Chaos Toolkit was chosen because it is free and open source and has a large ecosystem of extensions that allow you to fine-tune your chaos experiments to your own needs.[1] The Chaos Toolkit also uses a chaos experiment format that you specify using YAML or JSON.[2] As shown in the diagram in Figure 4-1, the toolkit takes your chaos experiment definition and orchestrates the experiment against your target system.

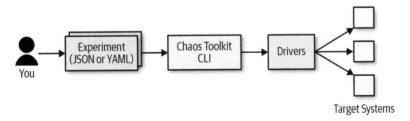

Figure 4-1. You use the Chaos Toolkit to orchestrate your chaos experiments against your target system

---

1 Disclaimer: the author cofounded the Chaos Toolkit project a couple of years ago.

2 The experiments used in this book will be in JSON format, but in the accompanying samples repository on GitHub (*http://bit.ly/2JbI6a7*) you will find the equivalent YAML experiment definitions as well.

Don't Sweat the Drivers

Don't worry about the drivers mentioned in Figure 4-1 for now. You'll learn all about Chaos Toolkit drivers in the following chapters when you use the toolkit to run experiments against various target systems. You'll even learn how to extend your Chaos Toolkit by creating your own custom drivers (see Chapter 8).

Now it's time to get the Chaos Toolkit installed. This means installing the Chaos Toolkit command-line interface (CLI), appropriately called chaos. With the chaos command installed, you can take control of your experiments by running them locally from your own machine.

Installing Python 3

The Chaos Toolkit CLI is written in Python and requires Python 3.5+. Make sure you have the right version of Python installed by running the following command and inspecting the output you get:

```
$ python3 -V
Python 3.6.4
```

If you don't have Python 3 on your machine (it is not bundled with macOS, for example), instructions for how to install it for your operating system are in the Chaos Toolkit documentation (*http://bit.ly/2LpvQ8A*).

Installing the Chaos Toolkit CLI

The Chaos Toolkit CLI adds the chaos command to your system so that you can:

- Discover and record what types of chaos and information can be sourced from your target system using the chaos discover command.

- Initialize new chaos experiments using the chaos init command.

- Execute your JSON- or YAML-formatted automated chaos experiments using the chaos run command.

- Optionally execute the report command to produce a human-readable report of your experiment's findings (see "Creating and Sharing Human-Readable Chaos Experiment Reports" on page 86).

Using these commands, you have the workflow shown in Figure 4-2 at your fingertips.

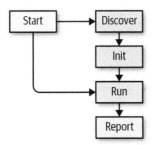

Figure 4-2. Starting with Discover, or jumping straight to Run, this is the workflow for the Chaos Toolkit

You should have Python successfully installed by now, so you're ready to install the Chaos Toolkit's `chaos` command. But first, to keep your environment neat and to avoid any Python module conflicts, it's a good idea to create a Python virtual environment just for the Chaos Toolkit and its supporting dependencies.

To create a Python virtual environment[3] (called `chaostk` in this example), use the following command:

```
$ python3 -m venv ~/.venvs/chaostk
```

Once the environment has been created, it needs to be *activated*. To activate the `chaostk` virtual environment, enter the following command:

```
$ source ~/.venvs/chaostk/bin/activate
```

Your command prompt will change to show that you are working in your new virtual environment by displaying the name of the virtual environment before the prompt:

```
(chaostk) $
```

Always Check Your Virtual Environment

I always check that I'm in the right virtual environment if the project I'm working on starts behaving oddly. It's easy to forget to activate an environment and start working with the Python and dependencies that have been installed globally, especially when you're changing between terminal windows, and even more so if you're new to Python.

---

3 You can delve into what Python virtual environments are and how they work in the official Python documentation (*http://bit.ly/31U1pNX*). A virtual environment is a nicely isolated sandbox in which you can control the Python dependencies and any other modules needed for a specific project without fighting module and dependency conflicts with other projects you are working on.

Finally, it's time to install the Chaos Toolkit chaos command. You can do this using the pip command (*https://pypi.org/project/pip*):

```
(chaostk) $ pip install chaostoolkit
```

After pip has successfully completed its work, you should have a shiny new chaos command to play with. For now, just check that all is present and correct by entering the chaos --help command:

```
(chaostk) $ chaos --help
chaos --help
Usage: chaos [OPTIONS] COMMAND [ARGS]...

Options:
  --version          Show the version and exit.
  --verbose          Display debug level traces.
  --no-version-check  Do not search for an updated version of the
                     chaostoolkit.
  --change-dir TEXT  Change directory before running experiment.
  --no-log-file      Disable logging to file entirely.
  --log-file TEXT    File path where to write the command's log.  [default:
                     chaostoolkit.log]
  --settings TEXT    Path to the settings file.  [default:
                     /Users/russellmiles/.chaostoolkit/settings.yaml]
  --help             Show this message and exit.

Commands:
  discover  Discover capabilities and experiments.
  init      Initialize a new experiment from discovered...
  run       Run the experiment loaded from SOURCE, either...
  validate  Validate the experiment at PATH.
```

chaos --help Output

The output of your chaos --help command may vary from the preceding output. It's rare that commands are added to the default Chaos Toolkit CLI, but over time it is possible.

Each of the commands in the Chaos Toolkit workflow contributes to the experimentation and validation phases of the Chaos Engineering Learning Loop (see Figure 4-3).

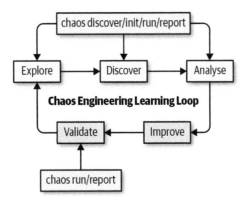

Figure 4-3. The Chaos Toolkit commands that support each of the phases of the Chaos Engineering Learning Loop

All of the commands that help you create and run chaos experiments (`discover`, `init`, `run`, `report`) are used when you are exploring and discovering weaknesses. The optional `report` command, not shown so far but discussed in Chapter 7, is there for when you are collaboratively analyzing a detected weakness. Finally, `run` and `report` are used again when you are validating that a weakness has been overcome.

Summary

Success! Your Chaos Toolkit is now successfully installed, and the `chaos` command is at your disposal. Now it's time to use that command.

In the next chapter, you'll bring to life a *very* simple system that will be a target for your chaos experiments. You'll then run your first chaos engineering experiment to complete a full turn of the Chaos Engineering Learning Loop.

Writing and Running Your First Automated Chaos Experiment

In Chapter 4 you grabbed the Chaos Toolkit; now it's time to actually *use* the toolkit to execute your first automated chaos experiment. In this chapter you'll set up a simple target system to work your chaos against, then write and run your first automated chaos experiment to surface a weakness in that system. You'll execute a whole cycle in which your automated chaos experiment is first used to uncover evidence of a weakness, and then used again to validate that the weakness has been overcome—see the diagram in Figure 5-1.

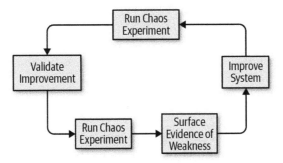

Figure 5-1. Using a chaos experiment to surface evidence of a weakness, then provide evidence of the weakness being overcome

Setting Up the Sample Target System

You need a system to explore for weaknesses, and everything you need for that is available in the *learning-chaos-engineering-book-samples* directory in the community-playground repo under the chaostoolkit-incubator organization. Grab the code now by cloning the repository with the git command:

```
(chaostk) $ git clone https://github.com/chaostoolkit-incubator/community-
            playground.git
```

If you're not comfortable with using git, you can simply grab the repository's contents as a zip file (*http://bit.ly/2NrGrCW*).

Getting the Example Code

In actual fact, *all* the experiments shown in this book are in the chaostoolkit-incubator/community-playground repo. For more information on the other contents in this repository, see Appendix B. For now, grab the Community Playground and keep it handy, as we're going to be using it throughout the rest of the book.

Once you've cloned the repository (or unpacked the zip file), you should see the following directory structure and contents in the *learning-chaos-engineering-book-samples* directory:

```
.
├── LICENSE
├── README.md
└── chapter5
    ├── experiment.json
    ├── resilient-service.py
    └── service.py

... further entries omitted ...
```

As you might expect, you'll be working from within the *chapter5* directory. Change directory in your terminal now so that you're in this directory (not forgetting to check that you still have your chaostk virtual environment activated).

A Quick Tour of the Sample System

Any chaos engineering experiment needs a system to target, and since this is your first experiment, the sample system has been kept very simple indeed. The key features of the system that is going to be the target of your chaos experiment are shown in Figure 5-2.

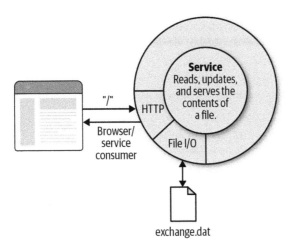

Figure 5-2. The single-service system that you'll be targeting with your first chaos experiment

The target system is made up of a single Python file, *service.py*, which contains a single runtime service with the following code:

```python
# -*- coding: utf-8 -*-
from datetime import datetime
import io
import time
import threading
from wsgiref.validate import validator
from wsgiref.simple_server import make_server

EXCHANGE_FILE = "./exchange.dat"


def update_exchange_file():
    """
    Writes the current date and time every 10 seconds into the exchange file.

    The file is created if it does not exist.
    """
    print("Will update to exchange file")
    while True:
        with io.open(EXCHANGE_FILE, "w") as f:
            f.write(datetime.now().isoformat())
        time.sleep(10)


def simple_app(environ, start_response):
    """
    Read the contents of the exchange file and return it.
    """
```

```
        start_response('200 OK', [('Content-type', 'text/plain')])
        with io.open(EXCHANGE_FILE) as f:
            return [f.read().encode('utf-8')]


if __name__ == '__main__':
    t = threading.Thread(target=update_exchange_file)
    t.start()

    httpd = make_server('', 8080, simple_app)
    print("Listening on port 8080....")

    try:
        httpd.serve_forever()
    except KeyboardInterrupt:
        httpd.shutdown()
        t.join(timeout=1)
```

This simple service deliberately does almost nothing of interest. It exposes an HTTP endpoint at its root, /, and serves the contents of a file, *exchange.dat*, when that URL is hit. To see the service in action, all you need to do is enter the following while in the *start* directory:

```
(chaostk) $ python3 service.py
Will update the exchange file
Listening on port 8080....
```

With the service running you should be able to visit *http://localhost:8080* and see the contents of the file that is served, as shown in Figure 5-3.

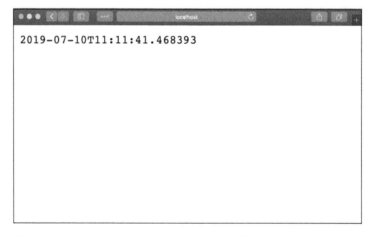

Figure 5-3. Try not to be too blown away by the incredible output from your target system's simple service…

To make things more interesting, in addition to serving the contents of the file the service also periodically refreshes the file's contents, so you should see the contents changing if you repeatedly hit *http://localhost:8080*.

What could possibly go wrong with such a trivial service? That is the question the team responsible for this service would ask when beginning to consider what chaos experiments might be interesting to explore. Worryingly, even in this trivial piece of code, there *is* a weakness—one that would result in service failure. And worse, it's a failure that would cascade directly to the service consumer.

Imagine for a moment that this is not such a trivial piece of code. Imagine that it is a business-critical service, part of a popular API, and that real customers rely on it—but there's a weakness! You may have already spotted it in such simple code, but for the sake of your first chaos engineering exercise, you'll now construct an experiment that will surface that weakness.

Exploring and Discovering Evidence of Weaknesses

Following the Chaos Engineering Learning Loop first shown in Figure 4-3, the initial step is to explore the target system to attempt to surface or discover any weaknesses (Figure 5-4).

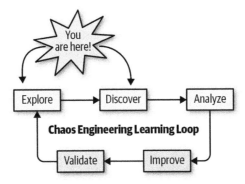

Figure 5-4. Using a chaos experiment to explore and discover weaknesses in the target system

The experiment is already written for you, using the declarative experiment specification format of the Chaos Toolkit.

Why the Experiment Specification?

Early in the design of the Chaos Toolkit, it was decided that collaboration, and therefore ease of communication, through chaos experiments was crucial. Most chaos engineering tools at the time concentrated on causing chaos, but none captured the real purpose of chaos engineering: the experiment itself.

Taking inspiration from the key concepts explained in *Chaos Engineering* (*http://bit.ly/2VliW0O*), by Casey Rosenthal et al. (O'Reilly), the Chaos Toolkit experiment specification was born. By containing those key chaos engineering concepts of the steady-state hypothesis, the method, and even optional rollbacks, the Chaos Toolkit experiment specification captures the chaos experiment vocabulary so that teams can collaborate, share, take inspiration from, and even entirely reuse experiment definitions across an organization or even between organizations.

The experiment is located in the *experiment.json* file, along with the *service.py* code. Open the *experiment.json* file in your favorite text editor, and you'll see that it starts with a title, a description, and some tags:

```
{
    "title": "Does our service tolerate the loss of its exchange file?",
    "description": "Our service reads data from an exchange file,
     can it support that file disappearing?",
    "tags": [
        "tutorial",
        "filesystem"
    ],
```

Every chaos experiment should have a meaningful title and a description that conveys how you believe the system will survive. In this case, you'll be exploring how the service performs if, or more likely when, the *exchange.dat* file disappears for whatever reason. The title indicates that the service should tolerate this loss, but there is doubt. This chaos experiment will empirically prove whether your belief in the resiliency of the service is well founded.

The next section of the experiment file captures the steady-state hypothesis. A steady-state hypothesis is:

> [A] model that characterizes the steady state of the system based on expected values of the business metrics.
>
> —*Chaos Engineering* (*http://bit.ly/2VliW0O*)

Remember that the steady-state hypothesis expresses, within certain tolerances, what constitutes *normal* and *healthy* for the portion of the target system being subjected to the chaos experiment. With only one service in your target system, the Blast Radius of your experiment—that is, the area anticipated to be impacted by the experiment— is also limited to your single service.

A Chaos Toolkit experiment's steady-state hypothesis comprises a collection of *probes*. Each probe inspects some property of the target system and judges whether the property's value is within an expected tolerance:

```
"steady-state-hypothesis": {
    "title": "The exchange file must exist",
    "probes": [
        {
            "type": "probe",
            "name": "service-is-unavailable",
            "tolerance": [200, 503],
            "provider": {
                "type": "http",
                "url": "http://localhost:8080/"
            }
        }
    ]
},
```

If all of the probes in the steady-state hypothesis are within tolerance, then the system is declared to be in a "normal," steady state.

Next comes the active part of an experiment, the experimental method:

```
"method": [
    {
        "name": "move-exchange-file",
        "type": "action",
        "provider": {
            "type": "python",
            "module": "os",
            "func": "rename",
            "arguments": {
                "src": "./exchange.dat",
                "dst": "./exchange.dat.old"
            }
        }
    }
]
```

A Chaos Toolkit experiment's method defines *actions* that will affect the system and cause the turbulent conditions, the chaos, that should be applied to the target system. Here the experiment is exploring how resilient the service is to the sudden absence of the *exchange.dat* file, so all the experiment's method needs to do is rename that file so that it cannot be found by the service.

As well as actions, the experiment's method can contain probes similar to those in the experiment's steady-state hypothesis, except without any tolerances specified. No tolerances are needed, as these probes are not assessing the target system. Rather, probes declared in the experiment's method enrich the output from an experiment's execution, capturing data points from the target system as the method is executed and adding those data points to the experiment's findings.

In this simple experiment definition, the method is the last section. There is one further section that is permitted, and that is the rollbacks section. You'll come to grips with rollbacks when you create more advanced experiments in Chapter 6.

Running Your Experiment

And now what you've been waiting for! It's time to execute your first chaos experiment and see whether the target system handles the chaos. You're now entering the discovery and analysis phases of the Chaos Engineering Learning Loop (Figure 5-5).

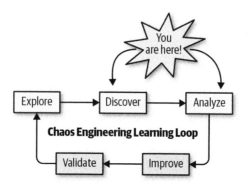

Figure 5-5. Using a chaos experiment to discover and begin to analyze any weaknesses surfaced in the target system

First make sure *service.py* is running in your terminal; you should see something like the following:

```
(chaostk) $ python3 service.py
Will update to exchange file
Listening on port 8080....
```

Now run your chaos experiment using the chaos run command in a new terminal window, making sure you have the chaostk virtual environment activated:

```
(chaostk) $ chaos run experiment.json
[2019-04-25 12:44:41 INFO] Validating the experiment's syntax
[2019-04-25 12:44:41 INFO] Experiment looks valid
[2019-04-25 12:44:41 INFO] Running experiment: Does our service tolerate the
loss of its exchange file?
[2019-04-25 12:44:41 INFO] Steady state hypothesis: The exchange file must exist
[2019-04-25 12:44:41 INFO] Probe: service-is-unavailable
[2019-04-25 12:44:41 INFO] Steady state hypothesis is met!
[2019-04-25 12:44:41 INFO] Action: move-exchange-file
[2019-04-25 12:44:41 INFO] Steady state hypothesis: The exchange file must exist
[2019-04-25 12:44:41 INFO] Probe: service-is-unavailable
[2019-04-25 12:44:41 CRITICAL] Steady state probe 'service-is-unavailable' is
not in the given tolerance so failing this experiment
```

```
[2019-04-25 12:44:41 INFO] Let's rollback...
[2019-04-25 12:44:41 INFO] No declared rollbacks, let's move on.
[2019-04-25 12:44:41 INFO] Experiment ended with status: failed
```

Congratulations! You've run your first automated chaos experiment. Even better, the terminal output indicates, through the CRITICAL entry, that you may have discovered a weakness. But before you start analyzing the potentially complex causes of the weakness, let's look at what the Chaos Toolkit did when it executed your chaos experiment.

Under the Skin of chaos run

The first job the Chaos Toolkit performs is to ensure that the indicated experiment is valid and executable. You can also verify this yourself *without* executing an experiment using the chaos validate command.

Assuming the experiment passes as valid, the Chaos Toolkit orchestrates the experiment execution based on your experiment definition, as shown in the diagram in Figure 5-6.

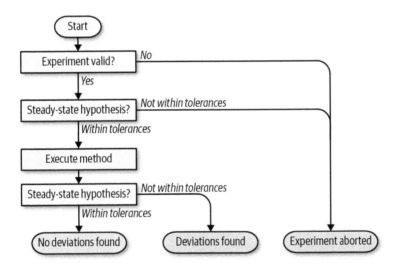

Figure 5-6. How the Chaos Toolkit interprets and executes an experiment

A surprising thing you'll notice is that the steady-state hypothesis is used twice: once at the beginning of the experiment's execution, and then again when the experiment's method has completed its execution.

The Chaos Toolkit uses the steady-state hypothesis for two purposes. At the beginning of an experiment's execution, the steady-state hypothesis is assessed to decide whether the target system is in a recognizably normal state. If the target system is deviating from the expectations of the steady-state hypothesis at this point, the experiment is aborted, as there is no value in executing an experiment's method when the target system isn't recognizably "normal" to begin with. In scientific terms, we have a "dirty petri dish" problem.

The second use of the steady-state hypothesis is its main role in an experiment's execution. After an experiment's method, with its turbulent condition–inducing actions, has completed, the steady-state hypothesis is again compared against the target system. This is the critical point of an experiment's execution, because this is when any deviation from the conditions expected by the steady-state hypothesis will indicate that there may be a weakness surfacing under the method's actions.

Steady-State Deviation Might Indicate "Opportunity for Improvement"

When a chaos experiment reports that there has been a deviation from the conditions expected by the steady-state hypothesis, you celebrate! This might sound odd, but any weakness you find in a target system *before* a user encounters it is not a failure; it's an opportunity for assessment, learning, and improvements in the resiliency of the system.

A glance at the *service.py* code will quickly highlight the problem:[1]

```
# -*- coding: utf-8 -*-
from datetime import datetime
import io
import time
import threading
from wsgiref.validate import validator
from wsgiref.simple_server import make_server

EXCHANGE_FILE = "./exchange.dat"


def update_exchange_file():
    """
    Writes the current date and time every 10 seconds into the exchange file.

    The file is created if it does not exist.
    """
    print("Will update to exchange file")
    while True:
        with io.open(EXCHANGE_FILE, "w") as f:
            f.write(datetime.now().isoformat())
```

---

1 If only it were this simple in large, complex systems! This assessment of the cause of a failure and a system weakness alone can take a lot of time when your system is bigger than one simple service.

```
            time.sleep(10)


    def simple_app(environ, start_response):
        """
        Read the content of the exchange file and return it.
        """
        start_response('200 OK', [('Content-type', 'text/plain')])
        with io.open(EXCHANGE_FILE) as f:
            return [f.read().encode('utf-8')]


    if __name__ == '__main__':
        t = threading.Thread(target=update_exchange_file)
        t.start()

        httpd = make_server('', 8080, simple_app)
        print("Listening on port 8080....")

        try:
            httpd.serve_forever()
        except KeyboardInterrupt:
            httpd.shutdown()
            t.join(timeout=1)
```

The code assumes that the *exchange.dat* file is *always there*. If the file disappears for
any reason, the service fails when its root URL is accessed, returning a server error.
Our experiment's title and description indicated that the presence of the file was not
guaranteed and that the service should be resilient to the condition of the file not
being present. The chaos experiment has proved that the service has been implemented without this resiliency in mind and shown that this condition will cause a
catastrophic failure in the service that will affect its consumers.

Improving the System

When a new weakness is surfaced by a chaos experiment's execution, it can often lead
to a lot of work that needs to be prioritized by the team responsible for the portion of
the system where the weakness has been found. Just analyzing the findings can be a
big job in itself!

Once you and your teams have conducted an analysis, it's time to prioritize and apply
system improvements to overcome any high-priority weaknesses (Figure 5-7).

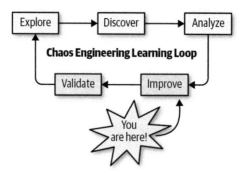

Figure 5-7. Once the challenge of analysis is done, it's time to apply an improvement to the system (if needed)

Fortunately, your target system contains only one simple service, and the weakness is relatively obvious in the service's *exchange.dat* file handling code.

An improved and more resilient implementation of the service is available in the *resilient-service.py* file:

```python
# -*- coding: utf-8 -*-
from datetime import datetime
import io
import os.path
import time
import threading
from wsgiref.validate import validator
from wsgiref.simple_server import make_server

EXCHANGE_FILE = "./exchange.dat"


def update_exchange_file():
    """
    Writes the current date and time every 10 seconds into the exchange file.

    The file is created if it does not exist.
    """
    print("Will update the exchange file")
    while True:
        with io.open(EXCHANGE_FILE, "w") as f:
            f.write(datetime.now().isoformat())
        time.sleep(10)


def simple_app(environ, start_response):
    """
    Read the contents of the exchange file and return it.
    """
```

```
        if not os.path.exists(EXCHANGE_FILE):
            start_response(
                '503 Service Unavailable',
                [('Content-type', 'text/plain')]
            )
            return [b'Exchange file is not ready']

        start_response('200 OK', [('Content-type', 'text/plain')])
        with io.open(EXCHANGE_FILE) as f:
            return [f.read().encode('utf-8')]


if __name__ == '__main__':
    t = threading.Thread(target=update_exchange_file)
    t.start()

    httpd = make_server('', 8080, simple_app)
    print("Listening on port 8080....")

    try:
        httpd.serve_forever()
    except KeyboardInterrupt:
        httpd.shutdown()
        t.join(timeout=1)
```

This more resilient service checks whether the *exchange.dat* file is present and, if not, responds with a more informative 503 Service Unavailable when the root URL of the service is accessed. This is a small and simple change, but it immediately improves the service such that it can gracefully deal with unexpected failure when accessing a file it depends on.

Validating the Improvement

It's now time to run your experiment again to validate that the improvement has overcome the discovered and analyzed weakness (Figure 5-8).

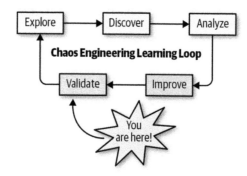

Figure 5-8. Your chaos experiment becomes a chaos test to detect whether the weakness has indeed been overcome

First ensure you've killed the original service instance that contained the weakness, and then run the new, improved, and more resilient service by entering:

```
$ python3 resilient-service.py
Will update to exchange file
Listening on port 8080....
```

Now switch to the terminal window where you previously ran your chaos experiment and run it again:

```
$ chaos run experiment.json
[2019-04-25 12:45:38 INFO] Validating the experiment's syntax
[2019-04-25 12:45:38 INFO] Experiment looks valid
[2019-04-25 12:45:38 INFO] Running experiment: Does our service tolerate the
loss of its exchange file?
[2019-04-25 12:45:38 INFO] Steady state hypothesis: The exchange file must exist
[2019-04-25 12:45:38 INFO] Probe: service-is-unavailable
[2019-04-25 12:45:38 INFO] Steady state hypothesis is met!
[2019-04-25 12:45:38 INFO] Action: move-exchange-file
[2019-04-25 12:45:38 INFO] Steady state hypothesis: The exchange file must exist
[2019-04-25 12:45:38 INFO] Probe: service-is-unavailable
[2019-04-25 12:45:38 INFO] Steady state hypothesis is met!
[2019-04-25 12:45:38 INFO] Let's rollback...
[2019-04-25 12:45:38 INFO] No declared rollbacks, let's move on.
[2019-04-25 12:45:38 INFO] Experiment ended with status: completed
```

Weakness overcome! The steady-state hypothesis does not detect a deviation in the target system, so you can celebrate that your chaos test has validated the improvement in system resiliency.

What Are the chaostoolkit.log and journal.json Files For?

You might have noticed that when you run the `chaos run` command, two new files appear after the experiment has finished executing: a *chaostoolkit.log* file and a *journal.json* file.

The *chaostoolkit.log* file is the raw log file of the toolkit's internal operations as it executes your experiment. It's useful for debugging the Chaos Toolkit itself.

The *journal.json* file is written when a chaos experiment completes and is a complete record of the entire execution of your experiment, including what experiment you used, what the return values were for the probes used in the steady-state hypothesis, and what the responses were to the actions in your experiment's method.

Although you *can* use the *journal.json* file directly, it's not exactly in the most human-readable form. This file is perfect for further interpretation and post-experiment execution by your own automation, but if you want to share your findings with other people, it's probably not what you're looking for. You'll see one use for the raw *journal.json* file in "Creating and Sharing Human-Readable Chaos Experiment Reports" on page 86, as you turn it into a useful findings report.

Summary

You've come a long way! In this chapter you've worked through a complete cycle: from surfacing evidence of a weakness all the way through to validating that the weakness has been overcome using your first automated chaos experiment. You've *explored*, *discovered* a weakness, *analyzed* that weakness, *improved* the system, and *validated* that the weakness has been overcome.

Now it's time to dive deeper into the Chaos Toolkit experiment definition vocabulary. In the next chapter you'll learn the details of the experiment definition format while you build your own chaos experiment from scratch.

## CHAPTER 6

Chaos Engineering from Beginning to End

In Chapter 5 you worked through an entire cycle, from discovery of system weaknesses to overcoming them using a preprepared automated chaos experiment. The Chaos Toolkit's experiment definition format is designed for this sort of sharing and reuse (see Chapter 7), but in this chapter you're going to build an experiment from first principles so that you can really experience the whole journey.

To make the challenge just a little more real, the weakness you're going to explore and discover against the target system in this chapter is multilevel in nature.

In Chapter 1 I introduced the many different areas of attack on resiliency, namely:

- People, practices, and processes
- Applications
- Platform
- Infrastructure

The experiment you're going to create and run in this chapter will look for weaknesses in both the *platform* and *infrastructure* areas, and even in the *people* area.

The Target System

As this experiment is going to examine weaknesses at the people level, you'll need more than a simple technical description of the target system. You'll still start, though, by enumerating the technical aspects of the system; then you'll consider the people, processes, and practices that will also be explored for weaknesses as part of the whole sociotechnical system.

The Platform: A Three-Node Kubernetes Cluster

Technically, the target system is made up of a Kubernetes cluster that is once again running nothing more than a simple service.

Kubernetes provides the *platform*, with Kubernetes nodes providing the lower-level infrastructure resources that support and run containers and services in the cluster. In this case, the target system has a three-node cluster topography.

Want More on Kubernetes?

A full description of all the Kubernetes concepts in play in a typical cluster is beyond the scope of this book. Check out the excellent, forthcoming *Kubernetes: Up and Running* 2nd Edition (*https://oreil.ly/2SaANU4*) by Kelsey Hightower et al. (O'Reilly) for a deeper dive into the platform.

So, for the purposes of your chaos experimentation in this chapter, there is going to be a service running on one or more replicated containers across a cluster made up of three nodes. Now it's time to describe and deploy that service to the cluster.

The Application: A Single Service, Replicated Three Times

Once again, you don't need a supercomplicated application made up of hundreds of services to have a system that is sufficiently complicated for weaknesses to be found. The application deployed onto your target system is going to be made up of a single service, defined as follows:

```
import platform

import cherrypy


class Root:
    @cherrypy.expose
    def index(self) -> str:
        return "Hello world from {}".format(platform.node())


if __name__ == "__main__":
    cherrypy.config.update({
        "server.socket_host": "0.0.0.0",
        "server.socket_port": 8080
    })
    cherrypy.quickstart(Root())
```

This code is available in the *chapter4/before* directory in the sample code for this book (*http://bit.ly/2JbI6a7*) that you grabbed earlier (see "Setting Up the Sample Target System" on page 46). Accompanying this service description is a description of the deployment itself:

```json
{
    "apiVersion" : "apps/v1beta1",
    "kind" : "Deployment",
    "metadata" : {
      "name" : "my-service"
    },
    "spec" : {
      "replicas" : 3,
      "selector" : {
        "matchLabels" : {
          "service" : "my-service"
        }
      },
      "template" : {
        "metadata" : {
          "name" : "my-app",
          "labels" : {
            "name" : "my-app",
            "service" : "my-service",
            "biz-app-id" : "retail"
          }
        },
        "spec" : {
          "containers" : [ {
            "name" : "my-app",
            "ports" : [ {
              "name" : "http",
              "containerPort" : 8080,
              "protocol" : "TCP"
            } ],
            "imagePullPolicy" : "Always",
            "image" : "docker.io/chaosiq/sampleservice:0.1.0",
            "resources" : {
              "limits" : {
                "cpu" : 0.1,
                "memory" : "64Mi"
              },
              "requests" : {
                "cpu" : 0.1,
                "memory" : "64Mi"
              }
            }
          } ]
        }
      },
      "strategy" : {
        "type" : "RollingUpdate",
        "rollingUpdate" : {
          "maxUnavailable" : 1,
```

```
            "maxSurge" : 1
          }
        }
      }
    }
```

The main thing to notice is the `replicas` directive in the *deployment.json* file. This directive specifies that the team that developed this service expects it to be run with three instances to provide a minimal fallback strategy should one or more of the replicas have a problem.

When you deploy these specifications, using a command such as `kubectl apply -f before/`, Kubernetes will establish a cluster where `my-service` will be replicated across the available nodes.

All good so far, but often there is more than one group of people involved in a system such as this. The service and deployment specifications represent the intent of the team responsible for the application itself, but there's typically another group responsible for the cluster itself, and that can lead to complications and turbulent conditions.

The People: Application Team and Cluster Administrators

In a system like this, there is often a dividing line between those who are responsible for managing a Kubernetes cluster, including all the real costs associated with these resources (let's call them the Cluster Administrators), and those trying to deploy and manage applications upon the cluster (the Application Team). The Cluster Administrators will be interested in tasks such as:

- Managing nodes
- Managing persistent disks
- Keeping an eye on the costs if these resources are hosted on a cloud provider
- Ensuring the cluster is not the problem, so they can go home for the weekend

The Application Team will be more focused on:

- Ensuring their application and its constituent services and third-party dependencies are healthy
- Ensuring they have enough redundancy and capacity across the Kubernetes pods being used to run their containers
- Ensuring they claim the persistent storage they need for their application to maintain its state
- Ensuring they can go home at 5:30 p.m. (other times are available)

The Application Team is responsible for making sure the *deployment.json* and *service.json* specifications ask for what they need from the platform. The Cluster Administrators will have their own dashboards and tools to ensure the underlying resources of the cluster are able to meet the needs expressed by the Application Team (see Figure 6-1).

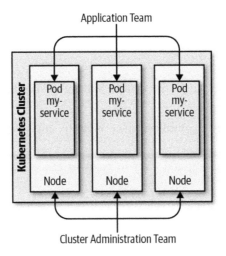

Figure 6-1. Application Team and Cluster Administrators working on a Kubernetes cluster

Hunting for a Weakness

At this point everything looks fine. The Application Team has defined what it needs, and the Cluster Administrators have provisioned enough resources to meet those needs. But you're a chaos engineer, so you're going to gather some empirical evidence to back up the trust and confidence everyone would like to have in this system.

You get the teams together to think about potential weaknesses in this system that could affect the reliability of the system as a whole. During this brainstorming session, you collaboratively notice a scenario that seems common enough, but no one is sure how it will play out on the production cluster.

The scenario is related to the split in responsibilities between the Cluster Administrators and the Application Team. During a regular working day, a Cluster Administrator may execute operations that cause issues with the goals of the Application Team. The situation that could possibly cause problems is one in which a Cluster Administrator takes action to remove a node from the cluster, for routine maintenance perhaps—this common action may leave the application in a state in which it cannot get access to the resources it needs (in this case, the required number of pods).

Through no fault of their own, the individual goals of the Cluster Administrators and the Application Team could end up in conflict, which could lead to system outages.

The challenge is that this scenario *could* be a problem, but you simply don't know for sure, and you can't know for sure until you test this case against the real system. It's time to kick off the *explore* phase of the Chaos Engineering Learning Loop so that you can try and *discover* whether there really is a weakness present.

For this automated chaos experiment, you will need to:

- Name your experiment
- Declare how you will know the system has not deviated from "normal" using a steady-state hypothesis
- Declare the turbulent conditions you want to apply to attempt to surface a weakness
- Declare any remediating actions you want to execute as rollbacks when your experiment is finished

Let's get started!

Naming Your Experiment

Create a new *experiment.json* file in your *chapter6* directory and start your experiment definition by considering how it should be named (I name chaos experiments according to the high-level question being explored). Then complete your title and description section with some tags:

```
{
    "version": "1.0.0",
    "title": "My application is resilient to admin-instigated node drainage",  ❶
    "description": "Can my application maintain its minimum resources?",  ❷
    "tags": [
        "service",
        "kubernetes"  ❸
    ],
```

❶ This is the statement of belief. You believe the system will be OK under the turbulent conditions explored in this experiment.

❷ The description gives you an opportunity to describe things in a little more detail, sometimes raising the doubt that's causing the experiment in the first place.

❸ Since we know we are targeting a Kubernetes-based system, it's helpful to others who might read and use our experiment to tag it as being applicable to that platform.

Defining Your Steady-State Hypothesis

What does "normal" look like? How should the system look so that you know it's operating within particular bounds? Everything may not be working, but the steady-state hypothesis isn't concerned with the health of the individual parts of a system; its main concern is that the system is still able to operate within declared tolerances, regardless of the turbulent conditions being injected through your experiment's method.

As we saw in Chapter 5, a steady-state hypothesis is made up of one or more probes and associated tolerances. Each probe will look for a property within your target system and judge whether that property's value is within the tolerance specified.

If *all* the probes declared in your steady-state hypothesis are within tolerance, then your system can be recognized as not in a "deviated" state. Define your steady-state hypothesis as the next section in your *experiment.json* file, as shown here:

```
"steady-state-hypothesis": {
    "title": "Services are all available and healthy", ❶
    "probes": [
        {
            "type": "probe",
            "name": "application-must-respond-normally",
            "tolerance": 200, ❷
            "provider": {
                "type": "http", ❸
                "url": "http://http://35.189.85.252/", ❹
                "timeout": 3 ❺
            }
        },
        {
            "type": "probe",
            "name": "pods_in_phase",
            "tolerance": true,
            "provider": {
                "type": "python", ❻
               -"module": "chaosk8s.pod.probes", ❼
                "func": "pods_in_phase", ❽
                "arguments": { ❾
                    "label_selector": "biz-app-id=retail",
                    "phase": "Running",
                    "ns": "default"
                }
            }
        }
    ]
},
```

❶ The title of your hypothesis should describe your belief in the normal condition of the system.

❷ The tolerance in this case expects the probe to return with a `200` status code.

❸ The first probe uses HTTP to assess the return value of an endpoint.

❹ You will need to change this value to the endpoint of the service as it is exposed from your Kubernetes cluster.

❺ A reasonable timeout is a good idea to ensure your experiment doesn't wait too long to decide that the system is normal.

❻ The second probe uses a call to a Python module.

❼ This is the name of the Python module to be used by this probe.

❽ This is the name of the Python function to be used by this probe.

❾ This is a key/value list of the arguments to be supplied to the probe's Python function.

This steady-state hypothesis shows you how a simple HTTP call can be used as a probe, or, if more complicated processing is necessary, how a Python module's function can be used instead. A third option that is not shown here is to use a call to a local process as a probe.

The Steady-State Is Used Twice

Don't forget: your steady state is used *twice* when an experiment is executed (see Figure 5-6): once at the beginning, to judge whether the target system is in a known and recognizably "normal" state in which to conduct your experiment; and once at the end, to detect whether there has been any observable deviation from what is known and recognizably "normal," which might indicate a system weakness.

In summary, your steady-state hypothesis for this experiment probes the target system to detect (a) that it is responding with an HTTP `200` status code within three seconds on the main entry point to the system and (b) that Kubernetes is reporting that all the pods within the system are in the healthy `Running` phase.

Now it's time to disrupt that with some turbulent conditions, declared in your experiment's method.

Injecting Turbulent Conditions in an Experiment's Method

A chaos experiment's method defines what conditions you want to cause in the effort to surface a weakness in the target system. In this case, your target system is a Kubernetes cluster. The challenge is that, out of the box, the Chaos Toolkit supports only a few limited and basic ways of causing chaos and probing a system's properties.

Installing the Chaos Toolkit Kubernetes Driver

By default, the Chaos Toolkit knows nothing about Kubernetes, but you can solve that by installing an extension called a *driver* (*http://bit.ly/2ZY67sd*). The Chaos Toolkit itself orchestrates your chaos experiments over a host of different drivers, which are where the real smarts are for probing and causing chaos in specific systems (see Chapter 8 for more on the different ways to extend the toolkit with your own drivers and CLI plug-ins).

Use the following `pip` command to install the Chaos Toolkit Kubernetes driver (*http://bit.ly/2xdwgXu*):

```
(chaostk) $ pip install chaostoolkit-kubernetes
```

That's all you need to add the capability to work with Kubernetes using the Chaos Toolkit. There is a growing list (*http://bit.ly/2ZY67sd*) of other open source and even commercially maintained drivers that are available as well, and later in this book you'll learn how to create your own driver; for now, though, all you need is the Kubernetes driver, and then you can use the toolkit to cause chaos from within your experiment's method.

Using the Kubernetes Driver from Your Method

A Chaos Toolkit driver provides a collection of probes and actions. Probes allow you to inspect the properties of your target system, either in support of a condition in your steady-state hypothesis or simply as a way of harvesting some useful information while your experiment is running. Actions are the turbulent condition–inducing parts of the driver.

For your experiment, you are taking on the role of a business-as-usual Kubernetes Cluster Administrator who is blissfully attempting to drain a node for maintenance reasons, unaware of the impact of this action on the needs of the application the cluster is running. Specifically, you're going to create an entry in your experiment's method that uses the `drain_nodes` action from the Kubernetes driver.

First you create a `method` block under the `steady-state-hypothesis` declaration in your experiment:

```
"steady-state-hypothesis": {
    // Contents omitted...
```

```
},
"method": [] ❶
```

❶ Your experiment's method may contain many actions and probes, so it is initial-
ized with a JavaScript array.

Now you can add your action. An action starts with a type that indicates whether this
is an action or a probe. If it is a probe, the result will be added to the experiment's
journal; otherwise, as an action it is simply executed, and any return value is ignored:

```
"steady-state-hypothesis": {
    // Contents omitted...
},
"method": [ {
    "type": "action",
}]
```

You can now name your action. You should aim to make this name as meaningful as
possible, as it will be captured in the experiment's journal when it records that this
action has taken place:

```
"steady-state-hypothesis": {
    // Contents omitted...
},
"method": [ {
    "type": "action",
    "name": "drain_node",
}]
```

Now it's time for the interesting part. You need to tell the Chaos Toolkit to use the
drain_nodes action from your newly installed Chaos Toolkit Kubernetes driver:

```
"steady-state-hypothesis": {
    // Contents omitted...
},
"method": [ {
    "type": "action",
    "name": "drain_node",
    "provider": { ❶
        "type": "python", ❷
        "module": "chaosk8s.node.actions", ❸
        "func": "drain_nodes", ❹
        "arguments": { ❺
            "name": "gke-disruption-demo-default-pool-9fa7a856-jrvm", ❻
            "delete_pods_with_local_storage": true ❼
        }
    }
}]
```

❶ The provider block captures how the action is to be executed.

❷ The `provider` in this case is a module written in Python.

❸ This is the Python module that the Chaos Toolkit is supposed to use.

❹ This is the name of the actual Python function to be called by this action.

❺ The `drain_nodes` function expects some parameters, so you can specify those here.

❻ You must specify the name of a current node in your cluster here. You can select a node from the list reported by `kubectl get nodes`.

❼ Node drainage can be blocked if a node is attached to local storage; this flag tells the action to drain the node even if this is the case.

And that's it—your experiment's method is complete, as the only action we're concerned with that *may* cause a weakness to surface is a Kubernetes Cluster Administrator doing their job by draining a node. At all times the conditions of the steady-state hypothesis should be within tolerance before and after this method has been executed if no weakness is present in the system.

Do All Extensions Have to Be Written in Python?

In short, no, extensions to the Chaos Toolkit do not need to be written in Python. The Chaos Toolkit was *designed for* extension, and so there are a few different ways you can implement your own drivers and plug-ins to integrate the toolkit into your tools and workflow.

Right about now you might be keen to run your experiment, but there is one more thing to consider. You will have caused turbulent conditions through your experiment's method that you may want to consider reversing. That's what an experiment's `rollbacks` section is for.

Being a Good Citizen with Rollbacks

The term "rollback" has different meanings depending on your background. For databases, it can mean anything from resetting a database and its data to a prior state to manually manipulating the data as it is reverted to ensure no data is lost.

In a chaos experiment, a rollback is simply a *remediating action*. It's something you know you can do to make your experiment a better citizen by re-establishing some system property that you manipulated in your experiment's method.

During your experiment so far, you have deliberately attempted to remove a Kubernetes node from active duty, just as Cluster Administrators may do in the course of their regular work. As you know you've made this change, it makes sense to try to revert it so that you can at least attempt to leave the system in a state similar to the one it was in before your experiment's method. You do this by defining a rollbacks section such as:

```
"rollbacks": [
    {
        "type": "action",
        "name": "uncordon_node",
        "provider": {
            "type": "python",
            "module": "chaosk8s.node.actions",
            "func": "uncordon_node", ❶
            "arguments": {
                "name": "gke-disruption-demo-default-pool-9fa7a856-jrvm" ❷
            }
        }
    }
]
```

❶ The uncordon_node function from the Chaos Toolkit's Kubernetes driver can be used to put back the node that was drained out of the cluster.

❷ Make sure you change the name of the node to match the one that was drained in your experiment's method. Once again, you can get the name of the node that you want to uncordon using kubectl get nodes.

To Roll Back or Not to Roll Back

While it's a good idea to at least attempt to revert changes you might have made in your experiment's method, doing so is by no means mandatory. You might be interested in observing how the turbulent conditions of an experiment affect the system over an extended period of time, in which case you might not have any remediating actions in your rollbacks section.

The same thinking affects the idea of having *automatic* rollbacks. We considered whether an experiment should make an attempt to automatically roll back any action by default. However, not only did this complicate the toolkit and the implementation of your drivers, but it also gave the wrong impression that a rollback is able to do its job entirely automatically; we wanted the chaos engineer to explicitly decide which actions are important and worthy of rolling back.

With your full experiment now complete, it's time to run it so that you can explore and discover what weaknesses may be present.

Bringing It All Together and Running Your Experiment

Before you run your experiment, it's a good idea to check that your target Kubernetes cluster is all set. You can use the `kubectl apply` command to set up the Application Team's services on your cluster:

```
$ kubectl apply -f ./before
```

This command will set up a single service with three pod instances that can serve the traffic for that service.

Make Sure You Have Configured Kubectl to Talk to the Right Cluster

The Chaos Toolkit Kubernetes driver uses whatever cluster is selected for your `kubectl` command as the cluster that it targets for your experiment's probes and actions. It's good practice to check that you're pointing at the right cluster target using `kubectl` before you run your experiment.

Now it's time to run your experiment that explores whether "My application is robust to admin-instigated node drainage," You can do this by executing the `chaos run` command (make sure you specify your experiment file's name if it's not *experiment.json*):

```
(chaostk) $ chaos run experiment.json
```

As the Chaos Toolkit explores your system using your experiment, you'll see the following output:

```
[2019-04-25 15:12:14 INFO] Validating the experiment's syntax
[2019-04-25 15:12:14 INFO] Experiment looks valid
[2019-04-25 15:12:14 INFO] Running experiment: My application is resilient to
admin-instigated node drainage
[2019-04-25 15:12:14 INFO] Steady state hypothesis: Services are all available
and healthy
[2019-04-25 15:12:14 INFO] Probe: application-must-respond-normally
[2019-04-25 15:12:14 INFO] Probe: pods_in_phase
[2019-04-25 15:12:14 INFO] Steady state hypothesis is met!
[2019-04-25 15:12:14 INFO] Action: drain_node
[2019-04-25 15:13:55 INFO] Action: drain_node
[2019-04-25 15:14:56 INFO] Steady state hypothesis: Services are all available
and healthy
[2019-04-25 15:14:56 INFO] Probe: application-must-respond-normally
[2019-04-25 15:14:56 INFO] Probe: pods_in_phase
[2019-04-25 15:14:56 ERROR]    => failed: chaoslib.exceptions.ActivityFailed: pod
'biz-app-id=retail' is in phase 'Pending' but should be 'Running' ❶
```

```
[2019-04-25 15:14:57 WARNING] Probe terminated unexpectedly, so its tolerance
could not be validated
[2019-04-25 15:14:57 CRITICAL] Steady state probe 'pods_in_phase' is not in the
given tolerance so failing this experiment ❷
[2019-04-25 15:14:57 INFO] Let's rollback...
[2019-04-25 15:14:57 INFO] Rollback: uncordon_node
[2019-04-25 15:14:57 INFO] Action: uncordon_node
[2019-04-25 15:14:57 INFO] Rollback: uncordon_node
[2019-04-25 15:14:57 INFO] Action: uncordon_node
[2019-04-25 15:14:57 INFO] Experiment ended with status: deviated
[2019-04-25 15:14:57 INFO] The steady-state has deviated, a weakness may have
been discovered
```

Success! Your experiment has potentially found a weakness: when you, as a Cluster Administrator, drained two nodes from the Kubernetes cluster, you left the system unable to honor the need for three instances (pods) of your service. Note that in this case you've rolled back the changes, but you could instead choose to leave the system degraded to observe what happens next.

One way of overcoming this weakness is to simply prevent a Cluster Administrator from being able to drain a node from the cluster when it would leave the requirements of the Application Team's services unsatisfied. You could do this by setting some rules for Cluster Administrators to follow, but there would always be the chance of someone making a mistake (humans, like all complex systems, are fallible!) Thus it might be useful to apply a policy to the system that protects it. That's what a Kubernetes Disruption Budget is for!

Stopping a Running Automated Chaos Experiment!

At some point you might want to stop an automated chaos experiment mid-execution if things start to go seriously wrong. You can control this sort of behavior using the Control concept in the Chaos Toolkit—see Part III for more on how to do this.

Overcoming a Weakness: Applying a Disruption Budget

A Kubernetes Disruption Budget (*http://bit.ly/2Yh3QrF*) limits the number of pods of a replicated application that are down simultaneously from voluntary disruption. Your experiment relies on the voluntary eviction of pods from the nodes that it is draining, so the Application Team can safeguard their pods and stop the Cluster Administrators from draining too many nodes at once by enforcing a Disruption Budget resource in the Kubernetes cluster:

```
{
        "apiVersion": "policy/v1beta1",
        "kind": "PodDisruptionBudget",
        "metadata": {
                "name": "my-app-pdb"
```

```
        },
        "spec": {
                "minAvailable": 3, ❶
                "selector": {
                        "matchLabels": {
                                "name": "my-app" ❷
                        }
                }
        }
}
```

❶ Specifies the *minimum* number of pods that must be in the READY state at a given moment in time.

❷ Selects the pods to be protected by this Disruption Budget.

Next, you can apply this Disruption Budget to your cluster by executing the following command:

```
$ kubectl apply -f ./after
```

Now you can use your very own chaos experiment as a test to ensure that the weakness detected before is no longer present.

Success (as a tester)! Your chaos-experiment-turned-test passes, as there is no deviation from the steady-state hypothesis, and thus the original weakness is not present.

Summary

In this chapter you've walked through the entire flow of creating an experiment, learning from it, and then using the experiment to test that the weakness that was found was overcome. But chaos experiments rarely get created and applied in a vacuum. It's now time to see how you can collaborate with others on your automated chaos experiments.

## CHAPTER 7

Collaborative Chaos

In Chapter 1 you learned that collaboration is key to successful chaos engineering. When you are running a chaos experiment, whether it be a Game Day or an automated experiment, *everyone* should be aware that chaos is happening (more on this in Chapter 10).

This collaboration also extends to your experiments and findings themselves. While you've seen how useful chaos engineering can be for you and your team as you surface, explore, and overcome weaknesses in your systems, it is potentially useful to others outside of your team as well.

The good news is that, because you put so much effort into defining hypotheses and experiments in those JSON or YAML documents with the Chaos Toolkit in earlier chapters, those experiments are almost ready to become useful candidates for cross-team sharing and even potential reuse. In this chapter you'll learn how to make a few final tweaks so that you can share and reuse your experiments as you write your own code.

But My Experiment Is Specific, There's No Value in Sharing It…

Even an experiment that is highly specific to a particular system can be of interest to people beyond those working on that system. Others could be inspired by everything from the type of experimental method being employed to the assumption made in your experiment's hypothesis. You can't predict when another person or team might be prompted to consider some potential weakness they hadn't thought of before simply by seeing the sorts of experiments you run against your system—so, whenever possible, always look to develop your experiments so that they can be shared.

Sharing Experiment Definitions

A few particular aspects of an experiment may stop it from being shareable embedded configuration values and, even worse, embedded secrets. You probably already know that it's a bad idea to share secrets in plain text in any of your development artifacts, and the same caution should be applied to your experiments. In addition, there likely are configuration values that could vary from system to system; externalizing those values is also good practice, so that anybody looking to directly reuse your experiment will be instructed of the configuration they will need to amend to do that.

Let's take a Chaos Toolkit chaos experiment candidate as an example (see Example 7-1).

Example 7-1. An experiment that contains embedded configuration and secrets

```
{
    "version": "1.0.0",
    "title": "Simply retrieves all events from Instana",
    "description": "Demonstrates retrieving all the events for a time window and
    adding them into the experiment's journal",
    "tags": [
        "instana"
    ],
    "secrets": {
        "instana": {
            "instana_api_token": "1234567789"
        }
    },
    "configuration": {
        "instana_host" : "http://myhost.somewhere"
    },
    "steady-state-hypothesis": {
        "title": "Services are all available and healthy",
        "probes": [{
                "type": "probe",
                "name": "app-must-respond",
                "tolerance": 200,
                "provider": {
                    "type": "http",
                    "url": "http://192.168.39.7:31546/invokeConsumedService"
                }
            }
        ]
    },
    "method": [
            {
            "type": "probe",
            "name": "get-all-events-in-window-from-instana",
            "provider": {
                "secrets": ["instana"],
```

```
            "type": "python",
            "module": "chaosinstana.probes",
                "func": "get_all_events_in_window",
                "arguments": {
                    "from_time": "5 minutes ago"
                }
            }
        }
    ],
    "rollbacks": []
}
```

This experiment helps to illustrate the two aspects we're looking to externalize: configuration and secrets. The experiment does nothing more than attach to the third-party Instana service (*https://www.instana.com*) and retrieve a collection of system events, which it then dutifully places in the experiment's output, the journal.

About This Experiment

This sample experiment actually comes from the Instana Chaos Toolkit driver's source code. Instana is an application performance management platform, and it's common to use a driver[1] that integrates with other tooling like this to inspect the state of an application as well as to provide observability around chaos experiments as they are executed (see Chapter 10).

There are some obvious `configuration` and `secrets` blocks that are needed to talk to Instana in the experiment method's single probe, and—dangerously in the case of secrets—the values are also specified in the experiment. In addition, the URL is specified for the `app-must-respond` probe in the experiment's steady-state hypothesis. The URL could vary from one environment to the next and thus would also be a worthy candidate for being made a configurable item.

To make this experiment more reusable, and *much* more shareable, you will:

- Move the URL for the `app-must-respond` probe into a configuration item.
- Move all of the experiment's configuration so that it is then sourced from the experiment's runtime environment.
- Move all of the experiment's secrets so that they are sourced from the experiment's runtime environment.

---

1 Or you can create your own driver—see Chapter 8.

Moving Values into Configuration

The `app-must-respond` probe's URL should really be declared as a configurable value so that your experiment can be pointed at different target systems. To do this, you create a new configuration item in the `configuration` block to contain the `application-endpoint` configurable property:

```
{
    ...

    "secrets": {
        "instana": {
            "instana_api_token": "1234567789"
        }
    },
    "configuration": {
        "instana_host" : "http://myhost.somewhere",
        "application_endpoint": "http://192.168.39.7:31546/
        invokeConsumedService"
    },
    "steady-state-hypothesis": {
        "title": "Services are all available and healthy",
        "probes": [{
                "type": "probe",
                "name": "app-must-respond",
                "tolerance": 200,
                "provider": {
                    "type": "http",
                    "url": "http://192.168.39.7:31546/invokeConsumedService"
                }
            }
        ]
    },

    ...
}
```

You can now refer to your new `application_endpoint` configuration property using its name wrapped in `${}` when it is needed in the `app-must-respond` probe:

```
{
    ...

    "steady-state-hypothesis": {
        "title": "Services are all available and healthy",
        "probes": [{
                "type": "probe",
                "name": "app-must-respond",
                "tolerance": 200,
                "provider": {
                    "type": "http",
                    "url": "${application_endpoint}"
```

```
                }
            }
        ]
    },

    ...
}
```

Introducing the `application_endpoint` configuration property is a good start, but it is still a hardcoded value in the experiment. The `instana_host` configuration property also suffers from this limitation. Adjusting the Instana host and your application endpoint for different environments would require the creation of a whole new experiment just to change those two values. We can do better than that by shifting those configuration properties into environment variables.

Specifying Configuration Properties as Environment Variables

A benefit of environment variables is that they can be specified and changed without affecting the source code of your experiments, making your experiments even more reusable. To make a configuration property populatable by an environment variable, you need to map an environment variable as containing the value for the configuration property using a key and value. This example shows the change for the `application_endpoint` property:

```
{
    ...

    "configuration": {
        "instana_host" : "http://myhost.somewhere",
        "application_endpoint": {
            "type" : "env",
            "key"  : "APPLICATION_ENDPOINT"
        }
    },

    ...
}
```

`type` specifies `env`, which tells the Chaos Toolkit to grab the value for this configuration property from the runtime environment. `key` then specifies the name of the environment variable that will supply that value.

Now you can do the same with the `instana_host` configuration property, leaving your experiment in a much better state—these two properties can then be configured at runtime depending on what Instana service is being used and where your application's endpoint is in that context:

```
{
    ...
```

```
    "configuration": {
        "instana_host" :
        {
            "type" : "env",
            "key"  : "INSTANA_HOST"
        }
        "application_endpoint": {
            "type" : "env",
            "key"  : "APPLICATION_ENDPOINT"
        }
    },
    ...
}
```

Externalizing Secrets

While externalizing configuration properties from experiments is good practice, externalizing secrets is *great* practice, if not absolutely essential. You should never have secrets embedded in your source code, and as automated chaos experiments are also code, it stands to reason that the same rule applies there.

At the moment, you *do* have a secret: the `instana_api_token`, which is hanging around in your experiment's code, just waiting to be committed and shared with everyone by accident:

```
{
    ...

    "secrets": {
        "instana": {
            "instana_api_token": "1234567789"
        }
    },

    ...
```

The embedding of a secret like that is a major no-no, so let's rectify that now. You have a couple of options as to where secrets can be sourced from when using the Chaos Toolkit, but for simplicity's sake, let's change this embedded secret so that it is sourced from an environment variable, as you did with the experiment's configuration properties:

```
{
    ...

    "secrets": {
        "instana": {
            "instana_api_token": {
                "type": "env",
                "key": "INSTANA_API_TOKEN"
```

```
            }
        }
    },
```

Now the `instana_api_token` secret is being sourced from the `INSTANA_API_TOKEN` environment variable, and your experiment is ready to be shared safely.

Scoping Secrets

You might have noticed in the previous example that the `secrets` block has an additional level of nesting when compared with the `configuration` block:

```
{
    ...

    "secrets": {
        "instana": {
            "instana_api_token": {
                "type": "env",
                "key": "INSTANA_API_TOKEN"
            }
        }
    },
    "configuration": {
        "instana_host" :
        {
            "type" : "env",
            "key"  : "INSTANA_HOST"
        }
    },

    ...
```

The `configuration` block directly contains the `instana_host` configuration property, but the `instana_api_token` secret is captured in an additional `instana` block. This is because secrets in Chaos Toolkit experiments are scoped to a specific named container. When a secret is used in an experiment, you must specify which secrets container is to be made available to the activity. You can't specify the names of the secrets explicitly, but you can specify the named container that has the needed secrets:

```
{

        "type": "probe",

        "name": "get-all-events-in-window-from-instana",

        "provider": {

            "secrets": ["instana"],

            "type": "python",
```

```
            "module": "chaosinstana.events.probes",

            "func": "get_all_events_in_window",

            "arguments": {

                "from_time": "5 minutes ago"

            }

        }

    }
```

This added level of control for secrets is purposeful. What you don't see is that configuration properties are not only available to pass explicitly as values to your probes and actions but are also passed to every underlying driver and control that the Chaos Toolkit uses.

That works well for configuration, but it's the last thing you'd want with secrets. Suppose someone fooled into adding a custom extension into your Chaos Toolkit that disseminated secrets anywhere they chose; applying the same strategy as was applied with configuration would be trivial and dangerous![2]

This is why secrets are scoped in their own named containers that must be explicitly passed to the activities in which they are to be used, as shown here:

```
{
    ...
    "method": [
            {
            "type": "probe",
            "name": "get-all-events-in-window-from-instana",
            "provider": {
                "secrets": ["instana"],
                "type": "python",
                "module": "chaosinstana.probes",
                    "func": "get_all_events_in_window",
                    "arguments": {
                        "from_time": "5 minutes ago"
                    }
            }
        }
    ],
    ...
}
```

---

2 Of course, you would have had to install the malicious Chaos Toolkit extension, but it would be even better if you could avoid the danger altogether.

In this experiment snippet, the `get-all-events-in-window-from-instana` probe needs access to the secrets scoped in the `instana` secrets container, and so this is explicitly specified using the `secrets` property on the probe's provider.

Specifying a Contribution Model

Anyone who encounters a shared experiment will be able to tell the hypothesis being explored, the method being employed to inject turbulent conditions, and even any suggested rollbacks. Those things alone will be pretty valuable to them, even if they are just looking for inspiration for their own experiments against their own system.

One piece of the puzzle is still not being taken advantage of, though, and it's something that you had available to you in your Hypothesis Backlog (see Chapter 2) and that you added into your Game Day preparations (see Chapter 3). Your backlog and your Game Day plans both mentioned the *contributions* to trust and confidence that an experiment might make if it were employed as a Game Day or automated chaos experiment.

The Chaos Toolkit experiment format does allow you to specify this information as a "contribution model" for a given experiment:

```
{
    ...

    "contributions": {
        "availability": "high",
        "reliability": "high",
        "safety": "medium",
        "security": "none",
        "performability": "none"
    },

    ...
}
```

The experiment can declare a set of contributions, with each contribution rated as `none`, `low`, `medium`, or `high` depending on how much the experiment author thinks the experiment contributes trust and confidence to a particular system quality. The `low`, `medium`, and `high` values likely need little explanation, but `none` is usually a bit more surprising.

The `none` setting is available for when you want to be explicit that an experiment does *not* contribute any trust or confidence to a particular system quality. Not specifying the contribution to a system quality leaves the degree of trust and confidence that the experiment might bring to that quality up to the reader's interpretation. By specifying `none`, the experiment author is communicating clearly that there was no intention to add anything to trust and confidence in the specified system quality.

While specifying a contribution model adds even more information to help a reader's comprehension when the experiment is shared, that's not all a contribution model adds. It also has a part to play when the *results* of an experiment's execution are being shared, and to facilitate that, it's time to look at how to create an experimental findings report.

Creating and Sharing Human-Readable Chaos Experiment Reports

When you execute a Chaos Toolkit experiment, it produces a journal of everything found when the experiment ran (see Chapter 4). This journal is a complete record of everything about the experiment and its context as the experiment ran, but although it's captured in a JSON file, named *journal.json* (*http://bit.ly/2Yfrk04*) by default,[3] it's not the easiest thing for us humans to parse.

It would be much nicer if you could produce a human-readable report from the journal of an experiment's findings—and with the `chaostoolkit-reporting` plug-in (*http://bit.ly/2Yfrk04*), you can.

Creating a Single-Experiment Execution Report

The `chaostoolkit-reporting` plug-in extends the toolkit's `chaos` command with the `report` sub-command so that you can generate PDFs, HTML, and many other formats as well. Installing the plug-in (*http://bit.ly/2KJm01N*) takes some effort as it requires native dependencies to work, so here we're going to use the prepackaged Docker container of the Chaos Toolkit (*http://bit.ly/2YiClxJ*) instead, as it comes with the reporting plug-in already installed.

The first thing you need to do is to make sure that you have Docker installed for your platform (*https://dockr.ly/2xdWFnV*). Once you have Docker installed, you should see something like the following when you enter `docker -v` from your command line:

```
$ docker -v
Docker version 18.09.2, build 6247962
```

You might get a different version and build number, but as long as the command runs, you should be all set. Now you can download the prepackaged Chaos Toolkit Docker image:[4]

```
$ docker pull chaostoolkit/reporting
Using default tag: latest
latest: Pulling from chaostoolkit/reporting
```

---

3 You can amend this—see Appendix A.

4 This may take a little while, as the image is on the large side!

```
bf295113f40d: Pull complete
62fe5b9a5ae4: Pull complete
6cc848917b0a: Pull complete
053381643ee3: Pull complete
6f73bfabf9cf: Pull complete
ed97632415bb: Pull complete
132b4f713e93: Pull complete
718eca2312ee: Pull complete
e3d07de070a7: Pull complete
17efee31eaf2: Pull complete
921227dc4c21: Pull complete
Digest: sha256:624032823c21d6626d494f7e1fe7d5fcf791da6834275f962d5f99fb7eb5d43d
Status: Downloaded newer image for chaostoolkit/reporting:latest
```

Once you've downloaded and extracted the image you can locate a *journal.json* file from an experiment's execution and, from within the directory containing that file, run the following command to generate your own human-readable and shareable PDF-format report:

```
$ docker run \
    --user `id -u` \
    -v `pwd`:/tmp/result \
    -it \
    chaostoolkit/reporting
```

Running this docker command will produce, by default, a PDF report based on the single *journal.json* file in your current directory. It's that simple, but it gets even better. If you have access to a number of journals (maybe you've been collecting them over time based on a single experiment, or maybe you've collected them during the execution of many different experiments that target the same system), then you can use the chaos report command to consume all of those experimental-finding journals to give you an even more powerful report.

Creating and Sharing a Multiple Experiment Execution Report

To create a report based on multiple experimental-findings journals, you just need to feed references to all those files into the chaos report command—or in our case, into the following docker command (if you had a collection of journal files that each began with *journal-*, such as *journal-1.json* and *journal-2.json*):

```
$ docker run \
    --user `id -u` \
    -v `pwd`:/tmp/result \
    -it \
    chaostoolkit/reporting -- report --export-format=html5 journal-*.json report.html
```

This command will take all of the specified journals and produce one über-report, by default named *report.pdf*, ready for sharing. And an additional piece of value is added to the reports if you specified a contribution model in each of the contributing experiments. If you had a contributions block in each of the experiments that produced your journals, then you will see a number of overview charts in your newly created report that show a picture of how the collective experiments contributed to trust and confidence across a range of system qualities![5]

Summary

In this chapter you've looked at how it's crucial to enable collaboration around experiments, how experimental findings are recorded through *journal.json* files, and even how those files can be turned into valuable reports in various formats. In Chapter 8 you'll turn up the collaboration dial one notch further and see how and why you can customize your own automated chaos experiment platform with features that can be shared across your team and organization.

It's time to customize your Chaos Toolkit.

---

[5] These are important summaries for anybody responsible for the reliability of a system!

Creating Custom Chaos Drivers

No two systems are created the same, and there are as many failure conditions out there as there are system implementation choices. For example, you might choose any of the following options:

- Run on a virtual machine

- Run on dedicated hardware in your own data center

- Use a virtual network

- Use a hardwired network

- Use AWS, Azure, Google Cloud…(pick your own cloud infrastructure as a service provider!)

The list is almost endless, and that's just at the infrastructure level! When you consider the many options available at other levels, such as the platform and application levels, you face a combinatorial explosion of options that would likely stymie any thoughts of a common tool for automated chaos experiments.

The key here is that none of these choices are *wrong*; they are just different, and your unique context will be different, too. Not everyone is running Docker containers in Kubernetes, or serverless event-driven functions—and even if they were, there's still sufficient variation among the leading cloud providers to make adapting to each environment a challenge.

Then there are the choices that are special to your context. Even though many infrastructure, platform, and even application implementation decisions are being standardized and commoditized, it's still likely you have something different from others in the industry. Maybe you have a legacy COBOL application, or perhaps you've forked and amended an open source framework just enough for it to be quite different from anything else out there. Whatever your situation, you just might have something special that also needs to be interacted with when you run your chaos experiments.

Fortunately, the Chaos Toolkit has the capability for customization built into it.

In Chapter 7 you learned that there are two main ways to extend the Chaos Toolkit to meet your needs:[1]

- Custom drivers (*http://bit.ly/2XvIHwJ*) that include your own implementations of probes and actions to support your experiments
- Custom controls (*http://bit.ly/2SIjPiC*) that provide ways to integrate your toolkit with operational concerns such as observability,[2] or even human intervention[3]

A large and still-growing collection of open source extensions available in the Chaos Toolkit (*http://bit.ly/2FBRKSD*) and the Chaos Toolkit Incubator (*http://bit.ly/2UQ3x4D*) implement some or all of these different extension points. You should always check those resources before creating your own custom extension, but it is quite common to extend your toolkit for your own context's needs.

Let's look at how you can create a custom driver to create custom actions and probes that can then be called from the `steady-state-hypothesis`, `method`, or `rollbacks` section of your experiment.

Creating Your Own Custom Driver with No Custom Code

You can integrate your experiments with your own systems without any additional code by using either of the following options from your experiment's probes and actions:

Making HTTP calls
    You can call an HTTP endpoint from your experiment's probes and actions.

Calling a local process
    You can call a local process from your experiment's probes and actions.

---

1 There is a third extension point called a *plug-in*. Plug-ins extend the functionality of the Chaos Toolkit's CLI itself, often adding new sub-commands or overriding existing sub-commands of the chaos command. Creating your own plug-in is beyond the scope of this book, but if you are interested in taking advantage of this customization option, then a good example is the reporting plug-in (*http://bit.ly/2Yfrk04*) (see "Creating and Sharing Human-Readable Chaos Experiment Reports" on page 86).

2 See Chapter 10.

3 See Chapter 11.

Implementing Probes and Actions with HTTP Calls

You've seen how to call an HTTP endpoint from an experiment's probe before (see "Exploring and Discovering Evidence of Weaknesses" on page 49). In a basic case in which you simply want to invoke an HTTP endpoint using a GET request, you first specify that the type of your probe's provider is http:

```
{
    "type": "probe",
    "name": "application-must-respond-normally",
    "tolerance": 200,
    "provider": {
        "type": "http",

    }
}
```

Then you provide the URL that is to be invoked:

```
{
    "type": "probe",
    "name": "simple-http-call",
    "provider": {
        "type": "http",
        "url": "http://somehost"
    }
}
```

But what if you want to do more than a simple GET HTTP request? Not a problem—the http provider (*http://bit.ly/2XCBJWK*) allows you to specify the following:

method
The HTTP method to use; i.e., GET (the default), POST, DELETE, etc.

headers
A list of keys and values to be passed as headers in the HTTP request

arguments
A list of keys and values to be passed as the request's payload

There's a problem here, though. By default, an HTTP probe like the one you've specified here will hang indefinitely if there is a problem reaching or serving from the specified URL endpoint. To take control over this, you can specify a timeout, in seconds, on your http provider:

```
{
    "type": "probe",
    "name": "simple-http-call",
    "provider": {
        "type": "http",
        "url": "http://somehost",
```

```
            "timeout": 3
        }
    }
```

The return value from an HTTP probe is a collection of the HTTP status, the response headers, and the contents of the HTTP response. If your probe was declared inside of your experiment's `steady-state` hypothesis block, then you can examine the status code to see if it is one of a collection as the probe's `tolerance`:

```
"steady-state-hypothesis": {
    "title": "Services are all available and healthy",
    "probes": [
        {
            "type": "probe",
            "name": "application-must-respond-normally",
            "tolerance": 200,
            "provider": {
                "type": "http",
                "url": "http://192.168.99.100:32638/invokeConsumedService",
                "timeout": 3
            }
        }
    ]
}
```

It is possible that you might want to examine a lot more than just the HTTP response status when using an `http` provider–implemented probe in your steady-state hypothesis. Maybe you'd like to examine the contents of the response's body for specific information, or even examine the returning headers for something important to your judgment that the system is in a recognizably normal state. Unfortunately, the `http` provider doesn't allow such advanced introspection; if you need such power, it's worth switching to a `process` provider such as a bash script,[4] as described next. Alternatively, if much more programmatic control is needed, then you might consider implementing your own custom driver in Python (see "Creating Your Own Custom Chaos Driver in Python" on page 93).

Implementing Probes and Actions Through Process Calls

Similar to the `http` provider, there is a `process` provider (*http://bit.ly/2XAIbNM*) in the Chaos Toolkit that allows your experiment to call any arbitrary local process as part of the experiment's execution. This time you'll create an `action` activity that uses the `process` provider:

```
{
    "type": "action",
    "name": "rollout-application-update",
```

---

4 Perhaps calling something as simple and powerful as your own shell script, or even something more complicated, such as your own compiled program!

```
    "provider": {
        "type": "process"
    }
}
```

You specify the local process you want to invoke using path, and you can specify any arguments to be passed to the process by populating arguments:

```
{
    "type": "action",
    "name": "rollout-application-update",
    "provider": {
        "type": "process"
        "path": "echo",
        "arguments": "'updated'"
    }
}
```

The process provider is a powerful way of integrating your experiments with anything that can be called locally. It is especially useful when you already have an existing set of tools that probe and act on your system, and you simply want to add the higher-level abstraction of the experiment itself on top of their functionality.

The Power of the process Provider

The power of the process provider becomes really obvious when you work with people that have deep knowledge of a system but no knowledge of chaos engineering experiments. Often those people have a deep grasp of the scripts and programs that can be used to interact with a given system, but you have the knowledge of how to capture the exercise as a complete experiment.

In such a case there's no real need for your colleagues to learn the intricacies of experiment creation (unless they want to); instead, they can work with the tooling choices they are comfortable with, and you can simply use the process probe to hook into their work.

Creating Your Own Custom Chaos Driver in Python

Sometimes you just need the power of a full programming language and supporting ecosystem of libraries when creating your own custom probes and actions. This is when it's time to consider implementing your own Python extension to the Chaos Toolkit.

The first step is to make sure you are in the Python virtual environment (or global environment, if that's your preference) where your instance of the Chaos Toolkit is installed:

```
(chaostk) $ chaos --help
...
```

Here, you're using the chaos command provided by the chaostk virtual environment you created earlier (see Chapter 4).

For our current purposes, you're going to create a custom Python driver that begins to integrate with the Chaos Monkey for Spring Boot (*http://bit.ly/2JeRF8n*), another chaos engineering tool that allows you to inject all sorts of turbulent conditions into running Spring Boot applications.[5]

Drivers Are Perfect for Integrating with Existing Chaos Tools

Chaos drivers in the Chaos Toolkit were designed for the specific purpose of being able to integrate not only with target systems, but also with third-party chaos engineering tools. This is why there are now drivers for systems such as Toxiproxy and Gremlin. Both are very capable chaos-inducing systems in their own right, and the Chaos Toolkit makes it possible for you to add the experiment definitions to each tool, as well as to then pick the best of each for your own chaos engineering needs.

The requirement for your new Chaos Monkey for Spring Boot driver is to be able to provide a probe that can respond regardless of whether the Chaos Monkey for Spring Boot is enabled on a particular Spring Boot application instance.[6]

Why Not an Action?

There's nothing special about an action or a probe implemented in a Python driver for the Chaos Toolkit; both are simply Python functions. The only difference is that an action is usually called from an experiment's method to manipulate and inject turbulent conditions, and a probe is called to inspect some property without affecting the system it is interacting with. After completing the following sections, you will have all you need to create your own Python action functions as well as the probe that is being walked through.

---

5 This is why the Chaos Monkey for Spring Boot is referred to as an application-level chaos tool. It is implemented at the application level as opposed to the infrastructure or platform level, to support turbulent condition injection there. Application-level chaos-inducing tools are particularly useful when it is difficult to inject turbulent conditions into the other levels, such as when working with a serverless platform like AWS Lambda.

6 For sharp-eyed readers, a complete Chaos Toolkit driver for the Chaos Monkey for Spring Boot is already available in the Chaos Toolkit incubator. The following sections show how you could create your own driver, and give you all the steps you need to create a driver for your own integrations.

Creating a New Python Module for Your Chaos Toolkit Extension Project

The first step is to create a new Python module project to house your new extension code. You could do this manually, but there's also a Python Cookiecutter (*http://bit.ly/2xe7nLj*) template available that can get you set up with the necessary boilerplate code for your new module.

To install the Cookiecutter tool, enter the following, taking care to confirm that you have activated your Python virtual environment for the Chaos Toolkit:

```
(chaostk) $ pip install cookiecutter
```

Now you can create a new module called chaosmonkeylite with the following command, filling in the information for the various prompts as you go:

```
(chaostk) $ cookiecutter https://github.com/dastergon/cookiecutter-chaostoolkit.git
full_name [chaostoolkit Team]: your_name
email [contact@chaostoolkit.org]: your_email
project_name [chaostoolkit-boilerplate]: chaostoolkit-chaosmonkeylite
project_slug [chaostoolkit_chaosmonkeylite]: chaosmlite
project_short_description [Chaos Toolkit Extension for X.]: Chaos Toolkit Extension for the Chaos Monkey for Spring Boot
version [0.1.0]: 0.1.0
```

If everything has gone well you can now list the contents of your current directory and see the contents of your new *chaostoolkit-chaosmonkeylite* project:

```
(chaostk) $ tree chaostoolkit-chaosmonkeylite
chaostoolkit-chaosmonkeylite
├── CHANGELOG.md
├── LICENSE
├── README.md
├── chaosmlite
│   └── __init__.py
├── ci.bash
├── pytest.ini
├── requirements-dev.txt
├── requirements.txt
├── setup.cfg
├── setup.py
└── tests
    └── __init__.py
```

All good so far! Now you should be able to change into the *chaostoolkit-chaosmonkeylite* directory and install your new, empty extension module, which will be ready for development and testing:

```
(chaostk) $ cd chaostoolkit-chaosmonkey
(chaostk) $ pip install -r requirements-dev.txt -r requirements.txt
...
```

```
(chaostk) $ pip install -e .
...

(chaostk) $ pytest
Test session starts (platform: darwin, Python 3.6.4, pytest 3.3.0,
pytest-sugar 0.9.0)
cachedir: .cache
rootdir: /Users/russellmiles/chaostoolkit-chaosmonkeylite, inifile: pytest.ini
plugins: sugar-0.9.0, cov-2.5.1
Coverage.py warning: No data was collected. (no-data-collected)

 generated xml file: /Users/russellmiles/chaostoolkit-chaosmonkeylite/junit-
 test-results.xml

---------- coverage: platform darwin, python 3.6.4-final-0 ----------
Name                    Stmts   Miss  Cover   Missing
-----------------------------------------------------
chaosmlite/__init__.py      2      2     0%   3-5
Coverage XML written to file coverage.xml


Results (0.02s):
```

Watch Out for Naming Conflicts

If there is already a directory called *chaosmonkeylite* wherever you ran the cookiecutter command, then you will get a conflict, as the Cookiecutter tool expects to create a new directory and populate it from empty.

Adding the Probe

Now that you have a Python module project all set up and reachable from your installation of the Chaos Toolkit, it's time to add some features. The first feature required is to provide a probe that can respond regardless of whether the Chaos Monkey for Spring Boot is enabled on a particular Spring Boot application instance.

Practicing test-driven development, you can create the following test for this new probe in your **tests** module, in a file named *test_probes.py*:

```
# -*- coding: utf-8 -*-
from unittest import mock
from unittest.mock import MagicMock

import pytest
from requests import Response, codes

from chaosmlite.probes import chaosmonkey_enabled ❶
```

```
def test_chaosmonkey_is_enabled():
    mock_response = MagicMock(Response, status_code=codes.ok) ❷
    actuator_endpoint = "http://localhost:8080/actuator"

    with mock.patch('chaosmlite.api.call_api', return_value=mock_response) as
    mock_call_api:
        enabled = chaosmonkey_enabled(base_url=actuator_endpoint) ❸

    assert enabled ❹
    mock_call_api.assert_called_once_with(base_url=actuator_endpoint,
                                          api_endpoint="chaosmonkey/status",
                                          headers=None,
                                          timeout=None,
                                          configuration=None,
                                          secrets=None)
```

❶ Imports the chaosmonkey_enabled function from the chaosmlite module.

❷ Mocks out the expected response from the Chaos Monkey for Spring Boot API.

❸ While mocking out the call to the chaosmlite.api.call_api, returning an expected response for the Chaos Monkey for Spring Boot being enabled, calls the chaosmonkey_enabled probe function.

❹ Asserts that the response correctly identifies that the Chaos Monkey for Spring Boot is enabled.

Now if you run the pytest command, you should see the following failure:

```
(chaostk) $ pytest
...
E    ModuleNotFoundError: No module named 'chaosmlite.probes'
...
```

That seems fair—the test is trying to use probes that you haven't even written yet! To do that now, add the following code into a *probes.py* file in the *chaosmlite* module directory:

```
# -*- coding: utf-8 -*-
from typing import Any, Dict

from chaoslib.exceptions import FailedActivity
from chaoslib.types import Configuration, Secrets
from requests.status_codes import codes

from chaosmlite import api

__all__ = ["chaosmonkey_enabled"]
```

```
def chaosmonkey_enabled(base_url: str,
                        headers: Dict[str, Any] = None,
                        timeout: float = None,
                        configuration: Configuration = None,
                        secrets: Secrets = None) -> bool: ❶
    """
    Enquire whether Chaos Monkey is enabled on the
    specified service.
    """

    response = api.call_api(base_url=base_url,
                            api_endpoint="chaosmonkey/status",
                            headers=headers,
                            timeout=timeout,
                            configuration=configuration,
                            secrets=secrets) ❷

    if response.status_code == codes.ok:
        return True ❸
    elif response.status_code == codes.service_unavailable:
        return False ❹
    else:
        raise FailedActivity(
            "ChaosMonkey status enquiry failed: {m}".format(m=response.text)) ❺
```

❶ Declares the new probe function. The probe returns a Boolean. You can also see how secrets and configuration are made available to the probe function.

❷ Calls an underlying function that is responsible for constructing and actually calling the Chaos Monkey for Spring Boot API.

❸ Returns `True` (i.e., the Chaos Monkey for Spring Boot is enabled), if the call responds with an ok response status code.

❹ Returns `False` (i.e., the Chaos Monkey for Spring Boot is not enabled), if the call responds with a `service_unavailable` response status code.

❺ Raises a Chaos Toolkit core `FailedActivity` exception if there is an unexpected response code. `FailedActivity` does not abort the experiment, but instead is added as a note to the experiment's findings captured in the *journal.json* file.

To close the loop on the implementation, let's take a quick look at the underlying `api` module that is actually responsible for invoking the Chaos Monkey for Spring Boot API. The following code should be added to an *api.py* file in the chaosmlite module:

```
import json
from typing import Dict, Any

import requests
```

```
from chaoslib.types import Configuration, Secrets
from requests import Response


def call_api(base_url: str,
             api_endpoint: str,
             method: str = "GET",
             assaults_configuration: Dict[str, Any] = None,
             headers: Dict[str, Any] = None,
             timeout: float = None,
             configuration: Configuration = None,
             secrets: Secrets = None) -> Response:
    """ Common HTTP API call to Chaos Monkey for Spring Boot. Both actions and
    probes call the Chaos Monkey for Spring Boot REST API by using this function.
    :param base_url: Base URL of target application
    :param api_endpoint: Chaos Monkey for Spring Boot actuator endpoint
    :param method: HTTP method, default is 'GET'
    :param headers: Additional headers when calling the Chaos Monkey for
            Spring Boot REST API
    :param assaults_configuration: Assaults the configuration to change the
            Chaos Monkey for Spring Boot setting
    :param timeout: The waiting time before connection timeout
    :param configuration: Provides runtime values to actions and probes in
            key/value format. May contain platform-specific API parameters
    :param secrets: Declares values that need to be passed on to actions or
            probes in a secure manner; for example, the auth token
    :return: Return requests.Response
    """

    url = "{base_url}/{api_endpoint}".format(
        base_url=base_url, api_endpoint=api_endpoint)

    headers = headers or {}
    headers.setdefault("Accept", "application/json")

    params = {}
    if timeout:
        params["timeout"] = timeout

    data = None
    if assaults_configuration:
        data = json.dumps(assaults_configuration)
        headers.update({"Content-Type": "application/json"})

    return requests.request(method=method,
                            url=url,
                            params=params,
                            data=data,
                            headers=headers)
```

> ## Couldn't I Have Just Put the Code for the API Directly into My Probe?
>
> You could have put the code in the`api.py` `call_api` function directly into your chaos `monkey_enabled` function in *probes.py*, but that would have made it more difficult to mock out the different concerns being implemented, as well as mixing low-level API manipulation with the function contract that your probe represents.
>
> If this extension were to grow in complexity, you would likely see that the code contained in the `call_api` function was repeated across many of your probes and actions. Thus, it often makes sense for a Chaos Toolkit extension to implement this separation of concerns so that low-level, reusable API calls are prepared in an *api.py* module, while *probes.py* contains the actual probe functions that will be called from the experiments.

If you run `pytest` now, you should see the following:

```
(chaostk) $ pytest
Test session starts (platform: darwin, Python 3.6.4, pytest 3.3.0,
pytest-sugar 0.9.0)
cachedir: .cache
rootdir: /Users/russellmiles/chaostoolkit-chaosmonkeylite, inifile: pytest.ini
plugins: sugar-0.9.0, cov-2.5.1

  tests/test_probes.py::test_chaosmonkey_is_enabled ✓
  100% ▇▇▇▇▇▇
generated xml file: /Users/russellmiles/chaostoolkit-chaosmonkeylite/
junit-test-results.xml

---------- coverage: platform darwin, python 3.6.4-final-0 ----------
Name                      Stmts   Miss  Cover   Missing
---------------------------------------------------------
chaosmlite/api.py            17     11    35%   35-50
chaosmlite/probes.py         13      3    77%   32-35
---------------------------------------------------------
TOTAL                        32     14    56%

1 file skipped due to complete coverage.
Coverage XML written to file coverage.xml


Results (0.17s):
      1 passed
```

You can now call your new Python probe function from your experiments:

```json
{
    "type": "probe",
    "name": "is_chaos_enabled_in_the_monkey",
    "provider": {
        "type": "python",
```

```
        "module": "chaosmlite.probes", ❶
        "func": "chaosmonkey_enabled", ❷
        "arguments": {
            "base_url": "http://localhost:8080/activator"
        } ❸
    }
}
```

❶ Specifies that you want to use your new extension module's probes.

❷ The name of your probe function to call.

❸ Any arguments required by your new probe.

And that's it: you have a complete Chaos Toolkit extension module ready to be used in your experiments. Now that you've created this Chaos Toolkit extension module, you could simply share the code for your new module with your colleagues, and they could use it and improve on it by following the same steps to set it up for development usage. Alternatively, you could build and distribute the module using a system such as PyPi (*https://pypi.org*) so that others can use it with a single `pip` command.

Adding a Module to the Chaos Toolkit Incubator Project

You might also consider whether the world would benefit from your new module! If so, the Chaos Toolkit community would love to hear your proposal to add your module to the Chaos Toolkit Incubator project (*http://bit.ly/2UQ3x4D*). There, it would join a host of others that are being worked on by teams all around the globe.[7]

Summary

In this chapter we've taken a deep dive into how to extend the Chaos Toolkit to support integrations with other systems through the concept of a driver. You've seen how to write probes and actions using simple HTTP calls, or calls to local processes, and how to implement more complex interactions using a custom Python Chaos Toolkit module.

In the next chapter, you'll take the jump into operational concerns that your automated chaos engineering experiments need to participate in.

---

7 Just don't propose the Chaos Monkey for Spring Boot driver you've been working on in this chapter; that already exists!

Chaos Engineering Operations

Chaos and Operations

If chaos engineering were just about surfacing evidence of system weaknesses through Game Days and automated chaos experiments, then life would be less complicated. Less complicated, but also much less safe!

In the case of Game Days, much safety can be achieved by executing the Game Day against a sandbox environment and ensuring that everyone—participants, observers, and external parties—is aware the Game Day is happening.[1]

The challenge is harder with automated chaos experiments. Automated experiments could potentially be executed by anyone, at any time, and possibly against any system.[2] There are two main categories of operational concern when it comes to your automated chaos experiments (Figure 9-1):

Control

You or other members of your team may want to seize control of a running experiment. For example you may want to shut it down immediately, or you may just want to be asked whether a particularly dangerous step in the experiment should be executed or skipped.

Observation

You want your experiment to be debuggable as it runs in production. You should be able to see what experiments are currently running, and what step they have just executed, and then trace that back to how other elements of your system are executing in parallel.

---

1 See Chapter 3.

2 That is, any system that the user can reach from their own computer.

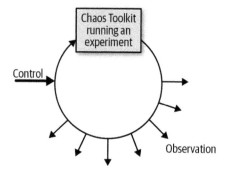

Figure 9-1. The control and observation operational concerns of a running automated chaos experiment

There are many implementations and system integrations necessary to support these two concerns, including dashboards, centralized logging systems, management and monitoring consoles, and distributed tracing systems; you can even surface information into Slack![3] The Chaos Toolkit can meet all these needs by providing both control and observation in one operational API (*http://bit.ly/2SIjPiC*).

Experiment "Controls"

A Chaos Toolkit control listens to the execution of an experiment and, if it decides to do so, has the power to change or skip the execution of an activity such as a probe or an action; it is even powerful enough to abort the whole experiment execution!

The control is able to intercept the control flow of the experiment by implementing a corresponding callback function, and doing any necessary work at those points as it sees fit. When a control is enabled in the Chaos Toolkit, the toolkit will invoke any available callback functions on the control as an experiment executes (see Figure 9-2).

---

3 Check out the free ebook *Chaos Engineering Observability* (*https://humio.com/chaos-observability*) I wrote for O'Reilly in collaboration with Humio for an explanation of how information from running experiments can be surfaced in Slack using the Chaos Toolkit.

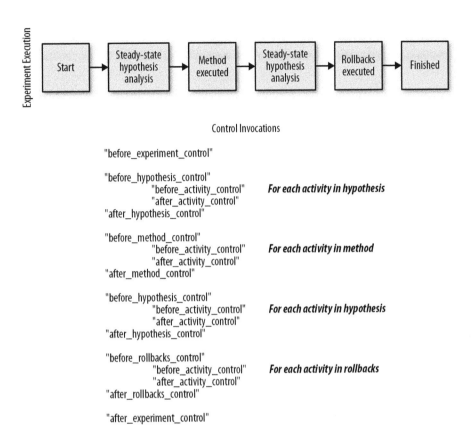

Figure 9-2. A control's functions, if implemented, are invoked throughout the execution of an experiment

Each callback function is passed any context that is available at that point in the experiment's execution. For example, the following shows the context that is passed to the `after_hypothesis_control` function:

```
def after_hypothesis_control(context: Hypothesis,
                             state: Dict[str, Any],
                             configuration: Configuration = None,
                             secrets: Secrets = None, **kwargs):
```

In this case, the steady-state hypothesis itself is passed as the context to the `after_hypothesis_control` function. The control's callback function can then decide whether to proceed, to do work such as sending a message to some other system, or even to amend the hypothesis if it is useful to do so. This is why a control is so powerful: it can observe *and* control the execution of an experiment as it is running.

A Chaos Toolkit control is implemented in Python and provides the following full set of callback functions:

```python
def configure_control(config: Configuration, secrets: Secrets):
# Triggered before an experiment's execution.
# Useful for initialization code for the control.
    ...

def cleanup_control():
# Triggered at the end of an experiment's run.
# Useful for cleanup code for the control.
    ...

def before_experiment_control(context: Experiment,
                        configuration: Configuration = None,
                        secrets: Secrets = None, **kwargs):
# Triggered before an experiment's execution.
    ...

def after_experiment_control(context: Experiment,
                        state: Journal, configuration:
                        Configuration = None, secrets:
                        Secrets = None, **kwargs):
# Triggered after an experiment's execution.
    ...

def before_hypothesis_control(context: Hypothesis,
                        configuration: Configuration = None,
                        secrets: Secrets = None, **kwargs):
# Triggered before a hypothesis is analyzed.
    ...

def after_hypothesis_control(context: Hypothesis, state:
                        Dict[str, Any], configuration:
                        Configuration = None, secrets:
                        Secrets = None, **kwargs):
# Triggered after a hypothesis is analyzed.
    ...

def before_method_control(context: Experiment,
                        configuration: Configuration = None,
                        secrets: Secrets = None, **kwargs):
# Triggered before an experiment's method is executed.
    ...

def after_method_control(context: Experiment, state: List[Run],
                        configuration: Configuration = None,
                        secrets: Secrets = None, **kwargs):
# Triggered after an experiment's method is executed.
    ...

def before_rollback_control(context: Experiment,
                        configuration: Configuration = None,
                        secrets: Secrets = None, **kwargs):
# Triggered before an experiment's rollback's block
```

```
# is executed.
    ...

def after_rollback_control(context: Experiment, state:
                            List[Run], configuration:
                            Configuration = None, secrets:
                            Secrets = None, **kwargs):
# Triggered after an experiment's rollback's block
# is executed.
    ...

def before_activity_control(context: Activity,
                              configuration: Configuration = None,
                              secrets: Secrets = None, **kwargs):
# Triggered before any experiment's activity
# (probes, actions) is executed.
    ...

def after_activity_control(context: Activity, state: Run,
                            configuration: Configuration = None,
                            secrets: Secrets = None, **kwargs):
# Triggered after any experiment's activity
# (probes, actions) is executed.
    ...
```

Using these callback functions, the Chaos Toolkit can trigger a host of operational concern implementations that could passively listen to the execution of an experiment, and broadcast that information to anyone interested, or even intervene in the experiment's execution.

Enabling Controls

By default, no controls are enabled when you run an experiment with the Chaos Toolkit. If a control implementation is present, it will not be used unless something enables it. A control can be enabled a few different ways:

- By a declaration somewhere in an experiment definition
- Globally so that it is applied to any experiment that instance of the Chaos Toolkit runs

Controls Are Optional

Controls are entirely optional as far as the Chaos Toolkit is concerned. If the Chaos Toolkit encounters a controls block somewhere in an experiment, the toolkit will try to enable it, but its absence is not considered a reason to abort the experiment. This is by design, as controls are seen as additional and optional.

Enabling a Control Inline in an Experiment

Enabling a control in your experiment definition at the top level of the document is useful when you want to indicate that your experiment ideally should be run with a control enabled:[4]

```
{
    ...

    "controls": [
        {
            "name": "tracing",
            "provider": {
                "type": "python",
                "module": "chaostracing.control"
            }
        }
    ],

    ...
```

You can also specify that a control should be invoked only for the steady-state hypothesis, or even only on a specific activity in your experiment.

Enabling a Control Globally

Sometimes you want to enable a control regardless of whether an experiment declares it. This can be done by adding the control to your *~/.chaostoolkit/settings.yaml* file:

```
controls:
    my-stuff:
        provider:
            type: python
            module: chaosstuff.control
```

Summary

In this chapter you've learned how a Chaos Toolkit control can be used to implement the operational concerns of control and observation. In the next chapter you'll look at how to use a Chaos Toolkit control to implement integrations that enable runtime observability of your executing chaos experiments.

---

4 "Ideally" because, as explained in the preceding note, controls in the Chaos Toolkit are considered optional.

## CHAPTER 10

Implementing Chaos Engineering Observability

In this chapter you're going to see how you can use existing Chaos Toolkit controls from the previous chapter to make your chaos experiments observable as they execute.

Observability is an important operational concern, because it helps you effectively debug a running system *without* having to modify the system in any dramatic way. You can think of observability as being a superset of system management and monitoring. Management and monitoring have traditionally been great at answering closed questions such as "Is that server responding?" Observability extends this power to answering open questions such as "Can I trace the latency of a user interaction in real time?" or "How successful was a user interaction that was submitted yesterday?"

When you execute automated chaos experiments, they too need to participate in the overall system's observability picture. In this chapter you're going to look at the following observability concerns and how they can be enabled for your own Chaos Toolkit chaos experiments:

- Logging the execution of your chaos experiments
- Distributed tracing of the execution of your chaos experiments

Adding Logging to Your Chaos Experiments

Centralized logging, made up of meaningful logging events, is a strong foundation of any system observability strategy. Here you're going to add your automated chaos experiment execution into your centralized set of logging events, adding events for all the different stages an experiment goes through when it is run.

You will implement a logging control that listens to a running chaos experiment and send events to a centralized logging system. You are going to see log events being pushed to the Humio centralized logging system, as that is one of the existing implementations available in the Chaos Toolkit Incubator.

The following code sample, taken from a full logging control (*http://bit.ly/2tcmz9G*), shows how you can implement a Chaos Toolkit control function to hook into the life cycle of a running chaos experiment:

```
...

def before_experiment_control(context: Experiment, secrets:
                              Secrets):
# Send the experiment

    if not with_logging.enabled:
        return

    event = {
        "name": "before-experiment",
        "context": context,
    }
    push_to_humio(event=event, secrets=secrets)

...
```

With the Humio extension installed (*http://bit.ly/2UMr4n6*), you can now add a con trols configuration block (see "Enabling Controls" on page 109) to each experiment that, when you execute it, will send logging events to your logging system:

```
{
    ...

    "secrets": {
        "humio": {
            "token": {
                "type": "env",
                "key": "HUMIO_INGEST_TOKEN"
            },
            "dataspace": {
                "type": "env",
                "key": "HUMIO_DATASPACE"
            }
        }
    },
    "controls": [
        {
            "name": "humio-logger",
            "provider": {
                "type": "python",
                "module": "chaoshumio.control",
                "secrets": ["humio"]
            }
        }
    ]
    ...
}
```

Alternatively, you can add a global entry into your \~/.chaostoolkit/settings.yaml file to enable the Humio control:

```
controls:
    humio-logger:
        provider:
            type: python
            module: chaosstuff.control
            secrets: humio
```

Centralized Chaos Logging in Action

Once that is configured, and the logging extension is installed, you will see logging events from your experiment arriving in your Humio dashboard, as shown in Figure 10-1.

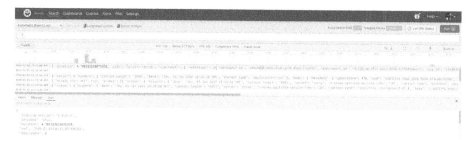

Figure 10-1. Chaos experiment execution log messages

Your chaos experiment executions are now a part of your overall observable system logging. Those events are now ready for manipulation through querying and exploring (see Figure 10-2), like any other logging events.

Figure 10-2. Querying chaos experiment executions

Tracing Your Chaos Experiments

Distributed tracing is critical to comprehending how an interaction with a running system propagates across the system. By enriching your logging messages with trace information, you can piece together the crucial answers to questions such as what events happened, in what order, and who instigated the whole thing. To understand how chaos experiments affect a whole system, you need to add your chaos experiments to the tracing observability picture.

Here you're going to see how you can use a Chaos Toolkit control that will be able to push trace information into distributed tracing dashboards so that you can view your chaos experiment traces alongside your regular system interaction traces.

Introducing OpenTracing

OpenTracing (*https://opentracing.io*) is a helpful open standard for capturing and communicating distributed tracing information.

The Chaos Toolkit comes with an OpenTracing extension (*http://bit.ly/2E1evyR*) that provides an OpenTracing control, and it's this control that you are going to use and see in action in this chapter.

Applying the OpenTracing Control

After you have installed the OpenTracing Chaos Toolkit extension (*http://bit.ly/2tbfsOP*), your experiments can be configured to use the OpenTracing control by specifying a `configuration` block:

```
{
    "configuration": {
        "tracing_provider": "jaeger",
        "tracing_host": "127.0.0.1",
        "tracing_port": 6831
    },
    "controls": [
        {
            "name": "opentracing",
            "provider": {
                "type": "python",
                "module": "chaostracing.control"
            }
        }
    ]
}
```

This configuration turns on the control and points the OpenTracing feed at a destination. The destination in this case is a Jaeger tracing visualization dashboard (*https://www.jaegertracing.io*), but it can be any tool that supports receiving an OpenTracing feed.

The preceding configuration tells the Chaos Toolkit to send an experiment execution's traces to the Jaeger dashboard, where those traces can be displayed alongside all the other traces in your runtime system, as shown in Figure 10-3.

Figure 10-3. Application and chaos traces in the Jaeger dashboard

Summary

In this chapter you used existing Chaos Toolkit controls to add logging and distributed tracing operational concerns to your automated chaos experiments. Both of these controls are *passive*; they simply listen to the execution of your experiment and send information off to their respective systems. Now it's time to create your own custom control—one that is *not* passive. Yours is going to provide real control over the execution of an experiment (refer back to Figure 9-1).

## CHAPTER 11

Human Intervention in Chaos Experiment Automation

So far you've created automated chaos engineering experiments that run from beginning to end. You kick off the experiment with `chaos run`, and when it is completed, you look at the output to see if there has been any deviation from the steady-state hypothesis that might indicate evidence of a possible system weakness.

For many automated chaos experiments, this execution strategy is perfect. Especially when you consider running chaos experiments continuously as tests (see Chapter 12), the capability of running experiments with no human intervention is essential.

Sometimes, though, more operational control is needed over the execution of a chaos experiment. Perhaps you have a probe activity in the steady-state hypothesis that you'd like to occasionally skip, or maybe there's an action activity in the experiment's method that you'd like to get a choice between continuing and executing or skipping in some cases. You might also want to introduce the ability to hit a metaphorical "Big Red Stop Button" so that you can choose to abort the experiment entirely if things start to go awry.

Each of these cases requires human intervention in the execution of your chaos experiments. The experiments will still be automated, but you want to allow someone to make choices about how an experiment is executed *as it is running*. All of these scenarios can be accomplished using the Chaos Toolkit's control feature.

Let's see how to do this now by creating two new Chaos Toolkit controls from scratch that introduce support for the following types of human interaction in your automated chaos experiment execution:

- A simple "Click to continue…"–style interaction

- An "Abort now!" user interaction that asks, at every step, whether you want to abort the whole experiment—otherwise known as the "Big Red Stop Button"

Creating a New Chaos Toolkit Extension for Your Controls

Just like Chaos Toolkit drivers, Chaos Toolkit controls are written in Python and usually placed within a Chaos Toolkit extension module. You could simply add your new controls to an existing Chaos Toolkit extension project—perhaps the one you created earlier for your custom Chaos Toolkit driver (see "Creating Your Own Custom Chaos Driver in Python" on page 93)—but to keep things clean and simple, you're going to create a new extension to contain your new controls.

As you did earlier, create a new Chaos Toolkit extension module using Cookiecutter (*http://bit.ly/2xe7nLj*):

```
(chaostk) $ cookiecutter \
         https://github.com/dastergon/cookiecutter-chaostoolkit.git
full_name [chaostoolkit Team]: your_name
email [contact@chaostoolkit.org]: your_email
project_name [chaostoolkit-boilerplate]: chaostoolkit-hci
project_slug [chaostoolkit_hci]: chaoshci
project_short_description [Chaos Toolkit Extension for X.]: Chaos Toolkit Extension \
that adds a collection of human interaction controls for automated \
chaos experiments.
version [0.1.0]: 0.1.0
```

Now you should have a new Chaos Toolkit extension within a *chaostoolkit-hci* directory:

```
(chaostk) $ tree chaostoolkit-hci
chaostoolkit-hci
├── CHANGELOG.md
├── LICENSE
├── README.md
├── chaoshci
│   └── __init__.py
├── ci.bash
├── pytest.ini
├── requirements-dev.txt
├── requirements.txt
├── setup.cfg
├── setup.py
└── tests
    └── __init__.py
```

Adding Your (Very) Simple Human Interaction Control

The first control you're going to add to your *chaostoolkit-hci* extension project is a simple "Click to continue..."-style interaction. The control will need to listen to the execution of any activity within the running experiment, pause and prompt the user with "Click to continue..." before each activity, and then continue when any key is pressed. Simple enough! In the *chaostoolkit-hci/chaoshci* directory, create a new file called *simplehci.py* with the following contents:

```
# -*- coding: utf-8 -*-
from chaoslib.types import Activity  ❶
import click

__all__ = ["before_activity_control"]

def before_activity_control(context: Activity, **kwargs):  ❷
    """
    Prompt to press a key before an activity is executed.
    """
    click.pause()  ❸
```

Here's what's happening in this code:

❶   The Chaos Toolkit provides a convenience type for any activity called `Activity`.

❷   You declare the single control callback method that you need to listen and act whenever *any* activity is about to be executed.

❸   Using the `click` Python library's `pause` function, you wait with the appropriate prompt for the user to press any key.

Now let's give this new control a spin. First you will need to install the `click` library, because it was not included by default when you generated the Chaos Toolkit extension project using Cookiecutter. To add the new dependency so that it is available at runtime, edit the *chaostoolkit-hci/requirements.txt* file so that it contains the following:

```
chaostoolkit-lib>=1.0.0
logzero
click
```

You can now install these dependencies by executing the following command in the *chaostoolkit-hci* directory:

```
(chaostk) $ pip install -r requirements.txt -r requirements-dev.txt
```

Before you can take your new control for a spin, you need to install the project as a Python module that can be reached by your Chaos Toolkit installation. You can use `pip` to do this by executing:

```
(chaostk) $ pip install -e .
...
Installing collected packages: chaostoolkit-hci
  Running setup.py develop for chaostoolkit-hci
Successfully installed chaostoolkit-hci
```

You can check that your new `chaostoolkit-hci` development code is ready and available by executing a `pip freeze`:

```
(chaostk) $ pip freeze
...
# Editable install with no version control (chaostoolkit-hci==0.1.0)
-e /Users/russellmiles/temp/chaostoolkit-hci
```

You're all set to give this control its first run! To do this, you need to have an experiment handy, so create a new file called *chaostoolkit-hci/samples/simple-interactive-experiment.json* and add this code to the file:

```
{
    "version": "1.0.0",
    "title": "A simple sample experiment that can be executed to show controls",
    "description": "Does nothing at all other than be executable \
                    by the Chaos Toolkit",
    "tags": [],
    "steady-state-hypothesis": {
```

```
        "title": "Assess the Steady State ... (not really in this case)",
        "probes": [
            {
                "type": "probe",
                "name": "hypothesis-activity",
                "tolerance": 0,
                "provider": {
                    "type": "process",
                    "path": "echo",
                    "arguments": "'updated'"
                }
            }
        ]
    },
    "method": [
            {
            "type": "action",
            "name": "method-activity",
            "provider": {
                "type": "process",
                "path": "echo",
                "arguments": "'updated'"
            }
        }
    ],
    "rollbacks": [
        {
            "type": "action",
            "name": "rollback-activity",
            "provider": {
                "type": "process",
                "path": "echo",
                "arguments": "'updated'"
            }
        }
    ]
}
```

This experiment doesn't actually do much other than contain activities in all of its major sections. The steady-state-hypothesis, method, and rollbacks sections each contain a single activity that simply echoes out some text. The main point here is to have an experiment in which you can showcase your new control.

Even though your new control is available, controls are disabled by default, so if you run this experiment now you won't see any of the interaction that you want the control to add:

```
(chaostk) $ chaos run samples/simple-interactive-experiment.json
[2019-04-25 12:02:58 INFO] Validating the experiment's syntax
[2019-04-25 12:02:58 INFO] Experiment looks valid
[2019-04-25 12:02:58 INFO] Running experiment: A simple sample experiment \
                           that can be executed to show controls
```

```
[2019-04-25 12:02:58 INFO] Steady state hypothesis: Assess the \
                           Steady State ... (not really in this case)
[2019-04-25 12:02:58 INFO] Probe: hypothesis-activity
[2019-04-25 12:02:58 INFO] Steady state hypothesis is met!
[2019-04-25 12:02:58 INFO] Action: method-activity
[2019-04-25 12:02:58 INFO] Steady state hypothesis: Assess the \
                           Steady State ... (not really in this case)
[2019-04-25 12:02:58 INFO] Probe: hypothesis-activity
[2019-04-25 12:02:58 INFO] Steady state hypothesis is met!
[2019-04-25 12:02:58 INFO] Let's rollback...
[2019-04-25 12:02:58 INFO] Rollback: rollback-activity
[2019-04-25 12:02:58 INFO] Action: rollback-activity
[2019-04-25 12:02:58 INFO] Experiment ended with status: completed
```

The experiment is running fine, but now it's time to enable your new human interaction control so that you can literally seize control of your experiment while it is running. You have a few different ways to enable a Chaos Toolkit control (see "Enabling Controls" on page 109), but first you need to add the control to each of the activities that you want to enable human interaction with. Edit your *simple-interactive-experiment.json* file so that it matches what's shown here:

```json
{
    "version": "1.0.0",
    "title": "A simple sample experiment that can be executed to show controls",
    "description": "Does nothing at all other than be executable \
                    by the Chaos Toolkit",
    "tags": [],
    "steady-state-hypothesis": {
        "title": "Assess the Steady State ... (not really in this case)",
        "probes": [
            {
                "type": "probe",
                "name": "hypothesis-activity",
                "tolerance": 0,
                "provider": {
                    "type": "process",
                    "path": "echo",
                    "arguments": "'updated'"
                },
                "controls": [
                    {
                        "name": "prompt",
                        "provider": {
                            "type": "python",
                            "module": "chaoshci.control"
                        }
                    }
                ]
            }
        ]
    },
    "method": [
```

```
            {
                "type": "action",
                "name": "method-activity",
                "provider": {
                    "type": "process",
                    "path": "echo",
                    "arguments": "'updated'"
                },
                "controls": [
                    {
                        "name": "prompt",
                        "provider": {
                            "type": "python",
                            "module": "chaoshci.control"
                        }
                    }
                ]
            }
        ],
        "rollbacks": [
            {
                "type": "action",
                "name": "rollback-activity",
                "provider": {
                    "type": "process",
                    "path": "echo",
                    "arguments": "'updated'"
                },
                "controls": [
                    {
                        "name": "prompt",
                        "provider": {
                            "type": "python",
                            "module": "chaoshci.control"
                        }
                    }
                ]
            }
        ]
    }
}
```

You've added an explicit controls block to each activity in your experiment. This should mean that those activities will now prompt the user to press any key to continue before they are executed. Test this now by executing your experiment:

```
(chaostk) $ chaos run samples/simple-interactive-experiment.json
[2019-04-29 11:44:05 INFO] Validating the experiment's syntax
[2019-04-29 11:44:05 INFO] Experiment looks valid
[2019-04-29 11:44:05 INFO] Running experiment: A simple sample experiment \
                           that can be executed to show controls
[2019-04-29 11:44:05 INFO] Steady state hypothesis: Assess the \
                           Steady State ... (not really in this case)
```

```
Press any key to continue ...
[2019-04-29 11:44:08 INFO] Probe: hypothesis-activity
[2019-04-29 11:44:08 INFO] Steady state hypothesis is met!
Press any key to continue ...
[2019-04-29 11:44:09 INFO] Action: method-activity
[2019-04-29 11:44:09 INFO] Steady state hypothesis: Assess the \
                           Steady State ... (not really in this case)
Press any key to continue ...
[2019-04-29 11:44:10 INFO] Probe: hypothesis-activity
[2019-04-29 11:44:10 INFO] Steady state hypothesis is met!
[2019-04-29 11:44:10 INFO] Let's rollback...
[2019-04-29 11:44:10 INFO] Rollback: rollback-activity
Press any key to continue ...
[2019-04-29 11:44:11 INFO] Action: rollback-activity
[2019-04-29 11:44:11 INFO] Experiment ended with status: completed
```

For each activity, including the second execution of the steady-state hypothesis's activity, you are prompted to continue. Success! However, in this simple case, it might be nicer not to have to specify the controls block for each activity. If *every* activity in an experiment will be subjected to a control, you can DRY things up a bit (*http://bit.ly/1RTzKPv*) by moving the controls block to the top level in the experiment, as shown in the following code:

```
{
    "version": "1.0.0",
    "title": "A simple sample experiment that can be executed to show controls",
    "description": "Does nothing at all other than be executable \
                    by the Chaos Toolkit",
    "tags": [],
    "controls": [
        {
            "name": "prompt",
            "provider": {
                "type": "python",
                "module": "chaoshci.simplehci"
            }
        }
    ],
    "steady-state-hypothesis": {
        "title": "Assess the Steady State ... (not really in this case)",
        "probes": [
            {
                "type": "probe",
                "name": "hypothesis-activity",
                "tolerance": 0,
                "provider": {
                    "type": "process",
                    "path": "echo",
                    "arguments": "'updated'"
                }
            }
        ]
```

```
        },
        "method": [
                {
                "type": "action",
                "name": "method-activity",
                "provider": {
                    "type": "process",
                    "path": "echo",
                    "arguments": "'updated'"
                }
            }
        ],
        "rollbacks": [
            {
                "type": "action",
                "name": "rollback-activity",
                "provider": {
                    "type": "process",
                    "path": "echo",
                    "arguments": "'updated'"
                }
            }
        ]
    }
```

Now when you run the experiment again, you'll see the same result as before but with far less code repetition.

How Can I Declare That a Control Should Be Applied to ANY Experiment I Run?

Sometimes you want a control to be applied to any experiment you might run with the Chaos Toolkit, regardless of whether it is explicitly declared in the experiment itself. To do this, you add your control to the Chaos Toolkit settings file (see "Enabling a Control Globally" on page 110).

That's your first control completed! Now let's go a bit further with another control that allows you to skip or execute individual activities in an experiment.

Skipping or Executing an Experiment's Activity

The next Chaos Toolkit control you're going to implement will provide a "Yes/No"–style interaction to run or skip a specific activity. You've seen just how simple it is to create a control; this will be just a small refinement! Add a new file to the *chaoshci* directory called *aborthci.py* and add the following code to it:

```
# -*- coding: utf-8 -*-
from chaoslib.types import Activity
```

```
from chaoslib.exceptions import InterruptExecution
import click
from logzero import logger

__all__ = ["before_activity_control"]


def before_activity_control(context: Activity, **kwargs):
    """
    Prompt to continue or abort the current activity.
    """
    logger.info("About to execute activity: " + context.get("name")) ❶
    if click.confirm('Do you want to continue the experiment?'): ❷
        logger.info("Continuing: " + context.get("name")) ❸
    else:
        raise InterruptExecution("Activity manually aborted!") ❹
```

❶ Here you add a logging message to indicate that an activity is about to be executed. This will be helpful to note if the activity is skipped.

❷ You're using the click library's confirm function, which asks a question and then
returns True to continue, or False if not.

❸ If the user indicates that the activity should be executed, then that is logged. Note
that you don't have to do anything else, simply carry on as normal.

❹ If the user indicates that they do not want to continue with the activity, but
instead want to skip it, then you take advantage of the InterruptException from
the Chaos Toolkit. This exception aborts the execution of the current activity but
still allows the experiment to continue to the next activity.

Copy your previous experiment in *samples/simple-interactive-experiment.json* into a
new experiment file called *samples/abortable-interactive-experiment.json* and enable
your new aborthci control in place of the existing simplehci control in the top-level
controls block:

```
{
    "version": "1.0.0",
    "title": "A simple sample experiment that can be executed to show controls",
    "description": "Does nothing at all other than be executable \
                    by the Chaos Toolkit",
    "tags": [],
    "controls": [
        {
            "name": "prompt",
            "provider": {
                "type": "python",
                // Here's where you switch to your new control
                "module": "chaoshci.aborthci"
```

```
            }
        }
    ],

    ... The remainder of the experiment stays the same.
```

Now execute your new experiment and control, electing to abort the experiment when asked the question for the method's activity:

```
(chaostk) $ chaos run samples/abortable-interactive-experiment.json
[2019-04-25 13:06:01 INFO] Validating the experiment's syntax
[2019-04-25 13:06:01 INFO] Experiment looks valid
[2019-04-25 13:06:01 INFO] Running experiment: A simple sample \
                            experiment that can be executed to show controls
[2019-04-25 13:06:01 INFO] Steady state hypothesis: Assess the \
                            Steady State ... (not really in this case)
[2019-04-25 13:06:01 INFO] About to execute activity: hypothesis-activity
Do you want to continue the experiment? [y/N]: y
[2019-04-25 13:06:03 INFO] Continuing: hypothesis-activity
[2019-04-25 13:06:03 INFO] Probe: hypothesis-activity
[2019-04-25 13:06:03 INFO] Steady state hypothesis is met!
[2019-04-25 13:06:03 INFO] About to execute activity: method-activity
Do you want to continue the experiment? [y/N]: N
[2019-04-25 13:06:04 CRITICAL] Experiment ran into an unexpected fatal error, \
                            aborting now.
    Traceback (most recent call last):
        ...
    chaoslib.exceptions.InterruptExecution: Experiment manually aborted!
[2019-04-25 13:06:04 INFO] Let's rollback...
[2019-04-25 13:06:04 INFO] Rollback: rollback-activity
[2019-04-25 13:06:04 INFO] About to execute activity: rollback-activity
Do you want to continue the experiment? [y/N]: y
[2019-04-25 13:06:06 INFO] Continuing: rollback-activity
[2019-04-25 13:06:06 INFO] Action: rollback-activity
[2019-04-25 13:06:06 INFO] Experiment ended with status: aborted
```

The experiment *is* aborted; your new control works as expected!

Aborting Does Not Cancel Execution of Rollback Activities

Raising the InterruptException does the trick of aborting the experiment, but you might have noticed that the activities in the rollbacks section are still attempted. Activities in the rollbacks section will always be executed, even if an experiment is aborted.

Summary

This chapter showed you how to seize control of an automated chaos experiment as it is running through the power of Chaos Toolkit controls. You developed two controls from scratch and tested how you could enable them in various ways, depending on whether they should be triggered on specific activities, across an entire experiment, or across all experiments globally

In the next chapter you will see how your experiments may eventually graduate into being valuable chaos *tests* that you can then choose to run continuously to build trust and confidence that the evidence of system weaknesses has not come back. It's time for *continuous chaos*!

## CHAPTER 12

Continuous Chaos

With every chaos experiment that you write and run, you increase your chances of finding evidence of dark debt that you can learn from and use to improve your system. Your chaos experiments will start out as explorations of your system; ways to ask yourself, "If this happens, I think the system will survive…or will it?" You'll gradually build a catalog of experiments for your system that explores a selection of your Hypothesis Backlog, helping you build trust and confidence that you're proactively exploring and surfacing weaknesses before they affect your users.

Some of your chaos experiments will then graduate into a different phase of their lives. The first phase of an experiment's life, as just described, is about *finding evidence* of system weaknesses. It's about exploring and uncovering that dark debt inherent in all complex sociotechnical systems. Over time, you will choose to overcome some or all of the weaknesses that your automated chaos experiments have surfaced evidence for. At that point, a chaos experiment enters the second phase of its life: it becomes a chaos *test*.

A chaos experiment is exploration; a chaos test is validation. Whereas a chaos experiment seeks to surface weaknesses and is celebrated when a deviation is found,[1] a chaos test validates that previously found weaknesses have been overcome.

There's more good news: a chaos experiment and a chaos test look *exactly the same*. Only the interpretation of the results is different. Instead of being a scientific exploration to find evidence of weaknesses, the goal has become to validate that those weaknesses seem to have been overcome. If a chaos engineer celebrates when evidence from a chaos experiment or Game Day shows that a new weakness may have been

---

1 Maybe "celebrate" is too strong a term for your reaction to finding potential evidence of system weaknesses, but that *is* the purpose of a chaos experiment.

found, they will celebrate again when no evidence of that weakness is found after that same experiment is run as a chaos test once system improvements have been put into place.

Over time you will build catalogs of hypotheses, chaos experiments (Game Days and automated experiments), and chaos tests (always automated). You'll share those experiments with others and demonstrate, through the contribution model (see "Specifying a Contribution Model" on page 85), what areas you are focusing on to improve trust and confidence in your system…but there is one more thing you could do to *really* turn those chaos tests into something powerful.

Chaos tests enable an additional chaos engineering superpower: they enable the potential for "continuous chaos."

What Is Continuous Chaos?

Continuous chaos means that you have regularly scheduled—often frequent—executions of your chaos tests. Usually chaos tests, rather than chaos experiments, are scheduled, because the intent is to validate that a weakness has not returned. The more frequently you schedule your chaos tests to run, the more often you can validate that a transient condition has not caused the weakness to return.

A continuous chaos environment is made up of these three elements:

Scheduler
    Responsible for taking control of when a chaos test can and should be executed

Chaos runtime
    Responsible for executing the experiment

Chaos tests catalog
    The collection of experiments that have graduated into being tests with a high degree of trust and confidence (see "Continuous Chaos Needs Chaos Tests with No Human Intervention" on page 131 for more on this)

Figure 12-1 shows how these three concepts work together in a continuous chaos environment.

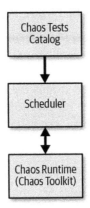

Figure 12-1. The key parts of a continuous chaos environment

Continuous Chaos Needs Chaos Tests with No Human Intervention

Chaos experiments commonly become chaos tests only when the weakness they detected through their deviation from the steady-state hypothesis is seen to be overcome (usually evidenced by running the experiment again) *and* when they do not require human intervention. In other words, a chaos experiment becomes a chaos test ready for continuous chaos once you are confident it shouldn't find any weaknesses *and* you are happy for it to run completely autonomously.

So far in this book you've been using the Chaos Toolkit as your chaos runtime, and you've been building up a collection of chaos experiments that are ready to be run as chaos tests; now it's time to slot the final piece into place by adding scheduled, continuous chaos to your toolset.

Scheduling Continuous Chaos Using cron

Since the Chaos Toolkit provides a CLI through the chaos command, you can hook it up to your cron scheduler.[2]

---

2 If you're running on Windows there are a number of other options, such as Task Scheduler.

Creating a Script to Execute Your Chaos Tests

We won't go into all the details of how to use cron here,[3] but it is one of the simplest ways of scheduling chaos tests to run as part of your own continuous chaos environment. First you need to have activated the Python virtual environment into which your Chaos Toolkit and its extensions are installed. To do this, create a *runchaos.sh* file and add the following to turn on your chaostk Python virtual environment (where your Chaos Toolkit was installed), and then run the chaos --help command to show that everything is working:

```
#!/bin/bash

source ~/.venvs/chaostk/bin/activate ❶

export LANG="en_US.UTF-8" # Needed currently for the click library
export LC_ALL="en_US.UTF-8" # Needed currently for the click library

chaos --help

deactivate ❷
```

❶ Activate the Python virtual environment where the Chaos Toolkit and any necessary extensions are installed.

❷ Deactivate the Python virtual environment at the end of the run. This is only included to show that you *could* activate and deactivate different virtual environments with different installations of the Chaos Toolkit and extensions depending on your experiment's needs.

Save the *runchaos.sh* file and then make it executable:

```
$ chmod +x runchaos.sh
```

Now when you run this script you should see:

```
$ ./runchaos.sh
Usage: chaos [OPTIONS] COMMAND [ARGS]...

Options:
  --version          Show the version and exit.
  --verbose          Display debug level traces.
  --no-version-check Do not search for an updated version of the
                     chaostoolkit.
  --change-dir TEXT  Change directory before running experiment.
  --no-log-file      Disable logging to file entirely.
  --log-file TEXT    File path where to write the command's log.  [default:
```

---

3 Check out *bash Cookbook* (*http://bit.ly/2tU1Sxg*) by Carl Albing and JP Vossen (O'Reilly) for more on using cron to schedule tasks.

```
                        chaostoolkit.log]
  --settings TEXT       Path to the settings file. [default:
                        /Users/russellmiles/.chaostoolkit/settings.yaml]
  --help                Show this message and exit.

Commands:
  discover  Discover capabilities and experiments.
  info      Display information about the Chaos Toolkit environment.
  init      Initialize a new experiment from discovered capabilities.
  run       Run the experiment loaded from SOURCE, either a local file or a...
  validate  Validate the experiment at PATH.
```

You can now add as many chaos run commands to the *runchaos.sh* script as you need to execute each of those chaos tests sequentially when the script is run. For example:

```
#!/bin/bash

source ~/.venvs/chaostk/bin/activate

export LANG="en_US.UTF-8" # Needed currently for the click library
export LC_ALL="en_US.UTF-8" # Needed currently for the click library

chaos run /absolute/path/to/experiment/experiment.json
# Include as many more chaos tests as you like here!

deactivate
```

This script will work well if your experiment files are always available locally. If that is not the case, another option is to direct the Chaos Toolkit to load the experiment from a URL.[4] You can do this by amending your *runchaos.sh* file with URL references in your chaos run commands:

```
#!/bin/bash

source ~/.venvs/chaosinteract/bin/activate

export LANG="en_US.UTF-8" # Needed currently for the click library
export LC_ALL="en_US.UTF-8" # Needed currently for the click library

chaos run /Users/russellmiles/temp/simpleexperiment.json
# Include as many more chaos tests as you like here!

deactivate
```

---

4 The specified URL must be reachable from the machine that the chaos run command will be executed on.

Adding Your Chaos Tests Script to cron

Now you can schedule a task with `cron` by adding an entry into your system's *crontab* (`cron` table). To open up the *crontab* file, execute the following:

```
$ crontab -e
```

This will open the file in your terminal's default editor. Add the following line to execute your *runChaosTests.sh* script every minute:

```
*/1 * * * * absolute/path/to/script/runChaosTests.sh
```

Save the file and exit, and you should see the `crontab: installing new crontab` message. Now just wait; if everything is working correctly, your chaos tests will be executed every minute by `cron`.

Scheduling Continuous Chaos with Jenkins

Scheduling your chaos tests to be executed every time there's been a change to the target system,[5] is a very common choice, so that's what you're going to set up now: you;ll install the popular open source Jenkins Continuous integration and delivery pipeline tool (*https://jenkins.io*) and add your chaos tests to that environment as an additional deployment stage.

Chaos Experiments in the Delivery Pipeline?

The goal of continuous chaos can easily lead you to think that you should include your chaos experiments and tests in your continuous delivery pipeline—the idea being that you could run your experiments and tests whenever you deploy new versions of the software, and if any weaknesses are detected in the new versions of the system, the deployment could be rolled back.

While there is value in using chaos tests this way, weaknesses in systems don't appear only at deployment time. Weaknesses can occur and be discovered by your chaos experiments and tests at any time, so scheduling your chaos experiment executions to run more frequently than your continuous delivery pipeline is often a good idea.

Grabbing a Copy of Jenkins

First you need to get a Jenkins server running, and the simplest way to do that is to download and install (*https://jenkins.io/download*) it locally for your operating

---

5 Possibly even as part of the choice to roll back during a blue-green deployment (*http://bit.ly/2FCDcBZ*).

---

system.[6] Once Jenkins has been downloaded, installed, and unlocked and is ready for work, you should see the Jenkins home screen shown in Figure 12-2.

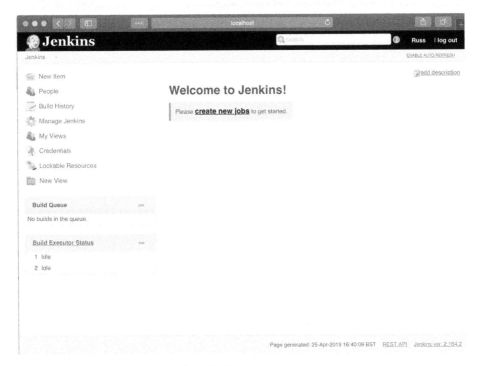

Figure 12-2. Jenkins installed and ready for use

Adding Your Chaos Tests to a Jenkins Build

You are now all set to tell Jenkins how to run your chaos tests. From the Jenkins home screen, click "create new jobs" (see Figure 12-2). You'll then be asked what type of Jenkins job you'd like to create. Select "Freestyle project" and give it a name such as "Run Chaos Tests" (see Figure 12-3).

---

6 If an instance of Jenkins is already available, please feel free to use that existing installation.

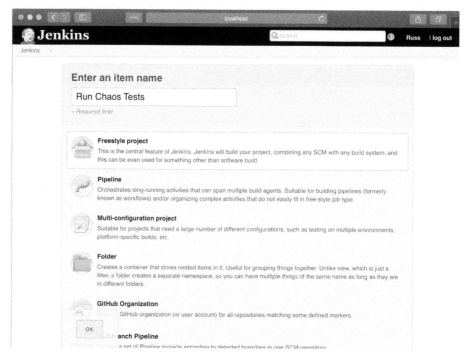

Figure 12-3. Create a new Jenkins freestyle project for your chaos tests

Once you've clicked OK to create your new project, you'll be presented with a screen where you can configure the job. There's a lot you could complete here to make the most of Jenkins, but for our purposes you're going to do the minimum to be able to execute your chaos tests.

Navigate down the page to the "Build" section and click the "Add build step" button (see Figure 12-4), and then select "Execute shell."

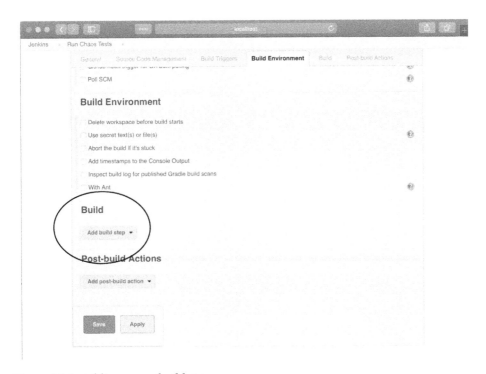

Figure 12-4. Adding a new build step

You'll be asked to specify the shell command that you want Jenkins to execute. You'll be reusing the *run-chaos-tests.sh* script that you created earlier, so simply enter the full path to your *run-chaos-tests.sh* file and then click "Save" (Figure 12-5).

Figure 12-5. Invoking the run-chaos-tests.sh shell script

You'll now be returned to your new Run Chaos Tests job page. To test that everything is working, click the "Build Now" link; you should see a new build successfully completed in the Build History pane (Figure 12-6).

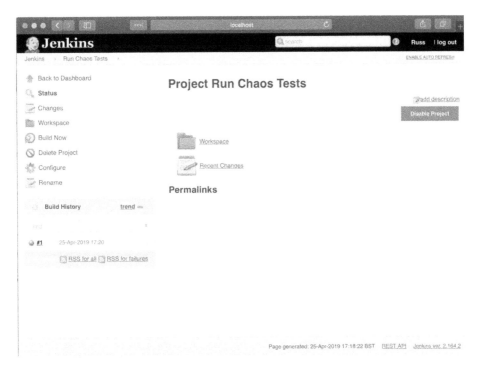

Figure 12-6. A successful single execution of your Run Chaos Tests job

You can see the output of running your chaos tests by clicking the build execution link (i.e., the job number) and then the "Console Output" link (Figure 12-7).

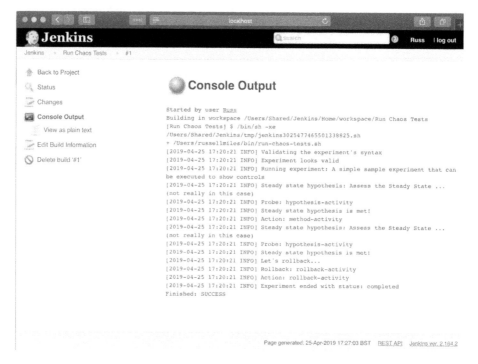

```
● ● ●  < >  ▢                     localhost              ⟳                    ↥  ⌷  +
  Jenkins                        🔍 search                          Russ   | log out
Jenkins  ·  Run Chaos Tests  ·  #1

  🏠 Back to Project
  🔍 Status                        ⚪ Console Output
  📃 Changes
  📇 Console Output               Started by user Russ
                                  Building in workspace /Users/Shared/Jenkins/Home/workspace/Run Chaos Tests
     View as plain text           [Run Chaos Tests] $ /bin/sh -xe
                                  /Users/Shared/Jenkins/tmp/jenkins3025477465501338825.sh
  📝 Edit Build Information        + /Users/russellmiles/bin/run-chaos-tests.sh
                                  [2019-04-25 17:20:21 INFO] Validating the experiment's syntax
  🚫 Delete build '#1'            [2019-04-25 17:20:21 INFO] Experiment looks valid
                                  [2019-04-25 17:20:21 INFO] Running experiment: A simple sample experiment that can
                                  be executed to show controls
                                  [2019-04-25 17:20:21 INFO] Steady state hypothesis: Assess the Steady State ...
                                  (not really in this case)
                                  [2019-04-25 17:20:21 INFO] Probe: hypothesis-activity
                                  [2019-04-25 17:20:21 INFO] Steady state hypothesis is met!
                                  [2019-04-25 17:20:21 INFO] Action: method-activity
                                  [2019-04-25 17:20:21 INFO] Steady state hypothesis: Assess the Steady State ...
                                  (not really in this case)
                                  [2019-04-25 17:20:21 INFO] Probe: hypothesis-activity
                                  [2019-04-25 17:20:21 INFO] Steady state hypothesis is met!
                                  [2019-04-25 17:20:21 INFO] Let's rollback...
                                  [2019-04-25 17:20:21 INFO] Rollback: rollback-activity
                                  [2019-04-25 17:20:21 INFO] Action: rollback-activity
                                  [2019-04-25 17:20:21 INFO] Experiment ended with status: completed
                                  Finished: SUCCESS


                                  Page generated: 25-Apr-2019 17:27:03 BST   REST API   Jenkins ver. 2.164.2
```

Figure 12-7. Console output from your chaos tests

Great! You now have Jenkins executing your chaos tests. However, your clicking the "Build Now" button is hardly "continuous." To enable continuous chaos, you need to add an appropriate *build trigger*.

Scheduling Your Chaos Tests in Jenkins with Build Triggers

You can trigger your new Run Chaos Tests Jenkins job in a number of different ways, including triggering on the build success of other projects. For our purposes, you can see some continuous chaos in action by simply triggering the job on a schedule, just as you did earlier with cron. In fact, Jenkins scheduled builds are specified with exactly the same cron pattern, so let's do that now.

From your Run Chaos Tests job home page, click "Configure" and then go to the "Build Triggers" tab (see Figure 12-8). Select "Build periodically" and then enter the same cron pattern that you used earlier when editing the crontab file, which was:

    */1 * * * *

Figure 12-8 shows what your completed build trigger should look like.

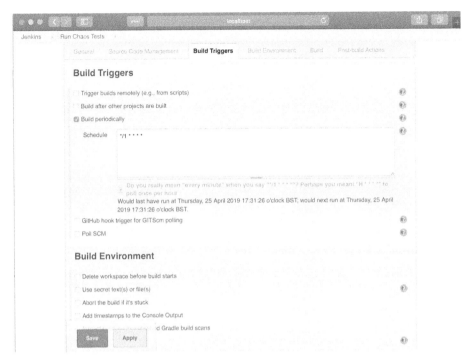

Figure 12-8. Configuring your Run Chaos Tests job to be triggered every minute

Now when you go back to your job's home page you should see new executions of your chaos tests being run every minute!

Summary

The progression from manual Game Days to automated chaos experiments to chaos tests and continuous chaos is now complete. By building a continuous chaos environment, you can search for and confidently surface weaknesses as often as needed, without long delays between Game Days.

But your journey into chaos engineering is only just beginning.

Chaos engineering never stops; as long as a system is being used, you will find value in exploring and surfacing evidence of weaknesses in it. Chaos engineering is never *done*, and this is a good thing! As a chaos engineer, you know that the real value of chaos engineering is in gaining evidence of system weaknesses as early as possible, so that you and your team can prepare for them and maybe even overcome them. As a mind-set, a process, a set of techniques, and a set of tools, chaos engineering is a part of your organization's resilience engineering capability, and you are now ready to play your part in that capability. Through the establishment of the learning loops that chaos engineering supports, everyone can be a chaos engineer and contribute to the reliability of your systems.

Good luck, and happy chaos engineering!

Chaos Toolkit Reference

The Chaos Toolkit is at its heart a simple CLI that introduces the chaos command.

The Default Chaos Commands

If you execute the chaos --help command once you've installed the Chaos Toolkit (see Chapter 4), you will see a list of the sub-commands that are supported:

```
(chaostk) $ chaos --help
Usage: chaos [OPTIONS] COMMAND [ARGS]...

Options:
  --version             Show the version and exit.
  --verbose             Display debug level traces.
  --no-version-check    Do not search for an updated version of the
                        chaostoolkit.
  --change-dir TEXT     Change directory before running experiment.
  --no-log-file         Disable logging to file entirely.
  --log-file TEXT       File path where to write the command's log.  [default:
                        chaostoolkit.log]
  --settings TEXT       Path to the settings file.  [default:
                        /Users/russellmiles/.chaostoolkit/settings.yaml]
  --help                Show this message and exit.

Commands:
  discover  Discover capabilities and experiments.
  info      Display information about the Chaos Toolkit environment.
  init      Initialize a new experiment from discovered capabilities.
  run       Run the experiment loaded from SOURCE, either a local file or a...
  validate  Validate the experiment at PATH.
```

This is the default set of sub-commands; you might see more than are listed here, especially if you've installed the reporting plug-in (see "Creating and Sharing Human-

Readable Chaos Experiment Reports" on page 86). They represent a workflow that goes a little beyond the chaos run command you've used throughout this book (see Figure A-1).

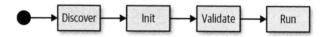

Figure A-1. The workflow for discover, init, validate, and run

Exploring the Options

You can also inspect all the options for the sub-commands by appending them with --help (for example, chaos discover --help).

You already know that you can use the chaos run command to execute your JSON or YAML format experiments. That works fine, and it's easily the most common command to use. The other commands are there to help you *author* your experiments, so let's take a deeper look at those now.

Discovering What's Possible with the chaos discover Command

One starting point when writing a new Chaos Toolkit experiment is the discover command. discover allows you to point your toolkit at an environment and have the toolkit try to discover what is there so that the information retrieved can be used to inform the generation of future experiments (see "Authoring a New Experiment with the chaos init Command" on page 146).

To show this in action, here's an example of using the discover command to inspect a Kubernetes target system and discover what is present:

```
(chaostk) $ chaos discover chaostoolkit-kubernetes
[2019-05-16 14:38:35 INFO] Attempting to download and install package \
                           'chaostoolkit-kubernetes'
[2019-05-16 14:38:36 INFO] Package downloaded and
                           installed in current environment
[2019-05-16 14:38:37 INFO] Discovering capabilities from chaostoolkit-kubernetes
[2019-05-16 14:38:37 INFO] Searching for actions
[2019-05-16 14:38:37 INFO] Searching for probes
[2019-05-16 14:38:37 INFO] Searching for actions
[2019-05-16 14:38:37 INFO] Searching for probes
[2019-05-16 14:38:37 INFO] Searching for actions
[2019-05-16 14:38:37 INFO] Discovery outcome saved in ./discovery.json
```

When executing the chaos discover command, you must supply the name of an extension to the Chaos Toolkit (in this case the Kubernetes extension chaostoolkit-kubernetes). This extension must in turn supply a discover function in its code, as it is this call that is used by the Chaos Toolkit. You can see an implementation of the discover function in the chaostoolkit-kubernetes driver (*http://bit.ly/2xdwgXu*):

```
def discover(discover_system: bool = True) -> Discovery:
    """
    Discover Kubernetes capabilities offered by this extension.
    """
    logger.info("Discovering capabilities from chaostoolkit-kubernetes")

    discovery = initialize_discovery_result(
        "chaostoolkit-kubernetes", __version__, "kubernetes")
    discovery["activities"].extend(load_exported_activities())
    return discovery
```

Nothing to Discover

Some extensions do not implement a discover function and thus will not return anything special when you refer to them with chaos discover.

When you execute chaos discover chaostoolkit-kubernetes, the Chaos Toolkit first checks whether the chaostoolkit-kubernetes Python module has been installed. If it hasn't, the toolkit will go ahead and attempt to install it.

Then the Chaos Toolkit will use the discover function to explore what is available in your currently configured Kubernetes environment. As you can see from the command output, the discover command constructs a view of your target system that can include:

Activities
    The probes or actions the extension can helpfully provide to work against the target system

System information
    A collection of information about the target system that can be helpful later when creating your experiments

All of this information is returned in a file that is called *discovery.json* by default. You can specify a different filename for your discovered information by passing the --discovery-path parameter to the chaos discover command.

You can open up your new *discovery.json* file and see the sorts of information returned for a given execution of chaos discover, but the real power of that file is that it is now used by the next step in the workflow: chaos init.

Authoring a New Experiment with the chaos init Command

The chaos discover command produces raw information about the system that you are targeting with your soon-to-be-written chaos experiment. With the *discovery.json* file in hand, you can now use the chaos init command to initialize a new experiment based on that discovered information:

```
(chaostk) $ chaos init
You are about to create an experiment.
This wizard will walk you through each step so that you can build
the best experiment for your needs.

An experiment is made up of three elements:
- a steady-state hypothesis [OPTIONAL]
- an experimental method
- a set of rollback activities [OPTIONAL]

Only the method is required. Also your experiment will
not run unless you define at least one activity (probe or action)
within it
Experiment's title:
...
```

The information provided from *discovery.json* is used by the chaos init command to present a wizard-style set of questions that talk you through the initial version of a new experiment. When you're finished, a new *experiment.json* file is generated for you to refine and execute.

Checking Your Experiment with the chaos validate Command

When you execute an experiment with chaos run, your experiment format is validated before any steps of the experiment are run. You can turn off this validation using the --no-validation switch, but most of the time it is still a valuable step.

When you're constructing a new experiment from scratch using the chaos discover and chaos init workflow, it can be useful to validate your experiment's format without the experiment being executed. You can achieve this with the chaos run command by providing the --dry switch, but it's cleaner to use the chaos validate command instead.

The combination of chaos discover, chaos init, and chaos validate exists to ease your experiment-creation life. With these tools at hand, you can quickly create JSON and YAML experiments for your Chaos Toolkit to execute.

Extending the Chaos Commands with Plug-ins

You can also extend the behavior of the chaos command using Chaos Toolkit plug-ins. This is great for when you want to introduce your own custom sub-commands beyond the out-of-the-box ones.

One example that you've already seen is the chaostoolkit-reporting plug-in (*http://bit.ly/2Yfrk04*). The Chaos Toolkit uses the click Python library (*http://bit.ly/2Ygc3ft*) to manage its commands, and the chaostoolkit-reporting plug-in extends the toolkit with the chaos report sub-command by implementing that command in a report method:

```
@click.command()
@click.option('--export-format', default="markdown",
              help='Format to export the report to: html, markdown, pdf.')
@click.argument('journal', type=click.Path(exists=True), nargs=-1)
@click.argument('report', type=click.Path(exists=False), nargs=1)
def report(export_format: str = "markdown", journal: str = "journal.json",
           report: str = "report.md"):
    """
    Generate a report from the run journal(s).
    """
    header = generate_report_header(journal, export_format)
    report_path = report
    reports = []

    if len(journal) == 1 and not os.path.isfile(journal[0]):
        journal = glob(journal)

    for journal in journal:
        reports.append(generate_report(journal, export_format))
    save_report(header, reports, report_path, export_format)
    click.echo("Report generated as '{f}'".format(f=report))
```

You can also add Chaos Toolkit CLI plug-in extensions to your own custom extension projects by implementing your own commands this way (see Chapter 8).

The Chaos Toolkit Community Playground

So, you've read this book and started your journey toward mastering chaos engineering. You've played with the included samples and seen how chaos experiments and Game Days can surface evidence of system weaknesses so that you can then prioritize what weaknesses should be learned from and addressed *before* they affect your users. It's a great start!

The next step might be more challenging. Before you start running your own Game Days and chaos experiments against your own systems you might want to practice a bit more. You might want to see others' experiments, and even how other systems have evolved in response to evidence of weaknesses. While nothing beats exploring a real system (sandbox or production) to learn about the evidence and insights that chaos engineering can provide, when you are taking your first steps it can be really helpful to work against smaller, simplified, safe systems while you get into the practice.

That is what the Chaos Toolkit Community Playground (*http://bit.ly/2JbI6a7*) is all about.

The Chaos Toolkit community has created the Community Playground as an open source and free project where you can explore different types of systems and accompanying chaos experiments. Each sample system in the playground includes a history through which you can see where an experiment has resulted in fundamental system improvements. This gives you a view of how chaos engineering can be used over time to surface evidence of weaknesses and then to validate that those weaknesses have been overcome in various deployments.

You already worked with the playground in exploring the sample code for this book. That code is continually evolving with new experiments and new strategies for overcoming system weaknesses. The Community Playground, where you can work with these experiments and systems alongside the rest of the community, is the best place to hone your chaos engineering skills. It's a safe place for you to take your own chaos engineering to the next level and share that experience with others.

You can also sign up for the chaostoolkit Slack channel (*https://join.chaostoolkit.org*), where the different sample applications and accompanying experiments in the Community Playground are discussed and maintained. Chaos engineering is a powerful discipline and practice, and the Chaos Toolkit Community Playground is the place for you to take the skills you've learned in this book to the next level.

On behalf of the entire Chaos Toolkit community, we look forward to seeing you there!

Index

About the Author

Russ Miles is the cofounder of the free and open source Chaos Toolkit, as well as CEO of the company behind the ChaosIQ project. For the past three years, Russ has been helping startups and enterprises surface and learn from weaknesses to improve the resiliency of their systems.

Colophon

The animal on the cover of *Learning Chaos Engineering* is a Geoffroy's spider monkey (*Ateles geoffroyi*), or black-handed spider monkey. The nineteenth-century French naturalist Étienne Geoffroy Saint-Hilaire gave the name *geoffroyi* to a handful of species he documented during research in the Americas. Geoffroy's spider monkeys are endangered due to habitat destruction. They live in Central America's coastal rain forests and mountain forests.

Black-handed spider monkeys have pale orange, rusty red, brown, or black fur on their bodies. As the name suggests, they have black fur from their hands to their elbows. These spider monkeys have unusually long fingers but only vestigial thumbs. Their arms and legs are notably long, too. Their whole bodies look slender, with arms longer than their legs and tails longer than their bodies. From head to tail, black-handed spider monkeys measure about three to five feet. They weigh between 13 and 20 pounds and feed primarily on ripe fruit.

In the upper canopy of forests, a black-handed spider monkey travels by *brachiation* —swinging from one arm to the other—as well as by walking, running, or climbing. When climbing and swinging, it uses its prehensile tail to grasp branches and vines as if it were an extra limb. Black-handed spider monkeys have been known to leap more than 30 feet in the canopy. They rarely come to the ground.

Perhaps that's why researchers have traced the development stages of their young to the position in which they're carried: females carry offspring in the womb for about 7.5 months, on their chests for one to two months after birth, and then on their backs intermittently for the first year. After one year, a spider monkey should be able to climb and swing by itself. To mate, females leave their family group and join another. An average female bears young every two to four years.

Geoffroy's spider monkey is a social species. Individuals live in *fission–fusion societies* of 20 to 40 members. The exact makeup of the group is dynamic, depending on time of day or activity. For example, when foraging for food, groups consist of two to six members. Black-handed spider monkeys have lived to 33 years in captivity, but their lifespan in the wild is unknown.

Many of the animals on O'Reilly covers are endangered; all of them are important to the world.

The cover illustration is by Karen Montgomery, based on a black-and-white engraving from Lydekker's *Royal Natural History*. The cover fonts are Gilroy Semibold and Guardian Sans. The text font is Adobe Minion Pro; the heading font is Adobe Myriad Condensed; and the code font is Dalton Maag's Ubuntu Mono.

O'REILLY®

There's much more where this came from.

Experience books, videos, live online training courses, and more from O'Reilly and our 200+ partners—all in one place.

Learn more at oreilly.com/online-learning